A Change of Allegiance

A journey into the historical and biblical
teaching of war and peace

Dean Taylor

Radical Reformation Books

Ephrata, Pennsylvania

Published by:
Radical Reformation Books
34 Cindia Ln.
Ephrata, PA 17522
www.RadicalReformation.com

ISBN: 0-9818973-0-4

Distributed by:
Scroll Publishing Company
P.O. Box 122
Amberson, PA 17210
(717) 349-7033
www.Scrollpublishing.com

Cover by:
Elizabeth Mong

Printed in the United States of America.

Table of Contents

Bonus

R
R
B

Radical Reformation Books
Ephrata, Pennsylvania

Forward

The year was 1991. It would be hard to say where it all really began...but there definitely had been a turning point about a year earlier. It was then that God's Spirit began to convict and move us in a powerful and life-changing way. As we made the commitment to follow Christ without compromise, we embarked on a journey that would forever change the course of our lives.

We had been soldiers stationed in Kaiserslautern, Germany; but now, we found ourselves leaving behind not only the country we had both grown to love, but also our citizenship in the world as we had always known it.

Join us on a journey and find out why we found Jesus' words so irresistible. Find out how we found the joyous simplicity of the Gospel not only liberating, but also empowering.

Throughout the book, I invite you to hear the stories of others who have gone before us. Their lives and testimonies far surpass our own. Shakespeare once said, "They speak true that breathe their words in pain." I assure you, after hearing the testimonies of the early church and the Anabaptist martyrs, you will never be the same.

My aim in writing this book is not simply to write one more book on the doctrine of nonresistance. My desire is to share with you some of my innermost thoughts; and how I struggled to find my way to the truths we now so freely embrace. Jesus said if we are ashamed of Him and His Words He will be ashamed of us in the end. In this book, I hope to challenge and inspire each reader to a higher and deeper devotion to

Him—to *hear* His living words and *do* His blessed will! Everything we need in this life is hidden in Him, and those who truly find *Him*—happy are they!

In short, there have been many, many Christian brethren living today who have blessed and influenced us with their teaching and testimonies of Christian integrity and faithful living. It would be impossible to list here everyone who has aided me in the writing of this book in one way or another. To each of you, I would like to express a heartfelt "Thank you"! May the Lord who sees in secret reward you openly!

However, I feel I must express my deepest thanks and appreciation to my dear wife, Tania, who not only shares this testimony with me, but has labored side-by-side with me in the writing of this book. Not only that, but if she had not willingly accompanied and supported me on the many difficult paths of this journey, I shudder to think whether there would be any testimony to give. I would also like to express my love and appreciation for our six wonderful children: Stephen, Stephana, Christian, Christina, Joanna, and John Wesley. You are living proof of God's mercy in my life!

Finally, I should mention that while this book is about nonresistance, my aim is not to make you passive, but rather, to make you a soldier—a soldier of the Kingdom of God. Furthermore, although this book is about non-violence, my prayer is that each page might be stained with the shed blood of Jesus.

I hope you enjoy the book. But mostly, I hope to convince you to give your allegiance—your life—your all—completely for Christ!

Chapter One

Walking on Dry Ground

Writing to Tania in Basic Training

It seemed like an eternity...

Slowly walking up the stairs, I felt like every step took a lifetime. While looking down to see if my camouflage uniform was pressed, my boots polished, and my buttons straight, I was rehearsing in my mind how in the world I was going to do this. What was I going to say? What was going to happen to us? Would he yell at us? Would we go to jail? There were so many unknowns.

I was tempted to fear. But my mind went to the biblical account of Israel at the Jordan River, how the waters did not recede until the feet of the Levites actually touched its banks. It was amazing; the closer I came to the door of our commander's office, the more my fears parted and I was able to walk in on God's grace, as on dry ground.

Just moments before we headed up the stairs, we had slipped away into a somewhat remote room to pray. We begged God for the grace and strength to walk in the light we had received. Getting up to our feet, we felt the empowerment of the Holy Spirit to go forward in confidence.

Our Army building was an old Nazi dance hall and brothel from the 1930s. For years I had hurried around this odd museum-like building without a thought. But now, slowly going up the stairs, I noticed the strata of chipped paint, the sounds of creaking wood and the peculiarly noisy clomping of leather boots as I led our small band of pilgrims up to face our commander. I was trembling, but God's grace was sufficient, and His Spirit quickened me.

Grabbing a person to serve as a witness on the way,

in one breath I forced a deep sigh, prayed a million prayers all at once, and then knocked on the commander's door. As "Chief" granted us permission to enter, we proceeded in file, stood at attention, and saluted. I then laid the packet containing the Army regulations on his desk.

"We are here to present our request for conscientious objector discharge, Sir…"

~Silence~

Our commander was a very curious man. Tall and lanky, he was usually very serious. He carried himself in a dignified way that seemed to command respect. Occasionally, you might get a dry joke out of him as he puffed from his pipe. But it seemed he was always in deep thought, forever gazing out somewhere just beyond the scope of congeniality and interpersonal connection. Certainly now, as we stood before him, there was no sign of levity or personal warmth.

Handing the thick packet of mimeographed Army papers to him, and trying to sound as confident as I could, I said, "Sir, you have before you Army Regulation 600-43. It deals with the rules and regulations that order the entire process for a soldier requesting conscientious objector discharge…"

~Big silence… as he slowly flipped through the record~

I've never been good with silence. Instead of savoring the seriousness of the moment, I often say something I probably shouldn't say—simply out of nervousness.

This moment was no exception…

Nervously, I blurted out, "Sir, I'm sorry if this is a shock to you. We don't mean to disgrace you or the unit, but we feel this is something we must do…"

~Still nothing…just quiet…he was still looking down, casually thumbing through the pages~

During the next few moments, I literally felt I might explode. My mind was racing. I wondered, "What will he say next?" "What *can* he say?"

Hardly looking up, he finally mumbled, "Okay, we will be sure to expedite this process as much as possible… You're dismissed."

As easy as that, we were headed back downstairs, wondering what was going to happen to us now. Returning to our unit, I felt an uneasy, sobering aura. It was a combination of the startling sensations of temporary normalcy and familiarity, mixed with the obvious deduction that my life was never going to be the same again. Without a doubt, it was the start of a long process that would forever change the course of my life.

Actually, these changes all had begun about a year earlier, when God had started working powerfully on my heart. My wife Tania and I were professional musicians in an Army band in Europe. Among other things, we were assigned to a rock band stationed in Germany. It was an unusual job. We would play concerts in officers' clubs, beer tents, music halls, and various military installations across Europe.

However, when we were serving back at our home base in Germany, my other job was serving as the unit armorer. This meant that I was in charge of the maintenance and distribution of the M-16 machine guns, M-203 grenade launchers, and various other weapons assigned to the soldiers of our unit. As far as Army assignments go, we had an exceptionally good one. We traveled all over Europe, and on occasion, we even played concerts for presidents and other dignitaries. We felt pretty strongly that we both would make a career of the Army band.

But that was before God intervened in our lives.

The changes really all began when my wife and I moved into the little village of Hochspeyer, just outside Kaiserslautern, Germany. By the providential hand of God, our house was situated deep in a valley not accessible to television reception. With this menacing distraction out of the way, we started to read the Bible together and have meaningful talks every night. During that time, God began to illuminate our minds, and subsequently our lives began to change. Through the Holy Spirit, God began to reveal many areas in our lives that were contrary to His Word. This awakening was profoundly specific and very sincere; it revealed to us that we were sinners, far from the heart of God.

Although we both thought we had known the Lord at one time, the Lord was making it clear to us just where we were spiritually, and it wasn't good. We were living a dangerous double life, caring little for the things of God. The rock band lifestyle was affecting all areas of our lives.

For a while I tried to appease my conscience by telling the guys in the band that I would not sing certain songs if they had obvious satanic or indecent lyrics. We had professed to be Christians, and these types of compromises had become pretty commonplace. They somehow made us feel better—for a while, anyway. Eventually, it became obvious to both of us that something had to change.

God was at work in our lives. The conviction of the Holy Spirit led us to a point of decision, and we both knew we could no longer go on as we had. Finally, one night in a hotel room while on tour in North Germany, we fell to our knees and totally surrendered our lives to Jesus Christ. As we rose to our feet, we both felt a firm resolve to live a life fully resigned to Christ from here on out, with "no compromise." That became somewhat of a banner to us—NO COMPROMISE. It has always been a challenge to keep this resolve.

Tania

I met my wife in high school. In so many ways, we grew up together. We were both musicians. Myself, a six-foot, three-inch sloppy and disorganized young man—and she, at five-foot, two inches, barely ninety-eight pounds and neat as a pin. We were opposites in many ways. However, early on in our relationship it became obvious that we were made for each other for the divine purpose of completing one another. Through the years, our love for each other has continued to grow. She is not only my wife; she is my spiritual companion, my confidant, and my best friend.

When these big changes started to happen to us in Germany, we had been married only a few years. Those early years of our marriage were years of deep introspection and intense challenges. In retrospect, it is clear that God specifically designed those years to shape us for His future use. How I thank God for my wife, my faithful companion through the years.

After we surrendered ourselves to Christ, one of the first areas in which we both felt God's specific leading concerned the nature of some of the music we were performing. Our Army rock band had regularly played in clubs and beer tents, all naturally bad environments. Eventually, we had even started to take jobs after hours at private bars and parties. It didn't take long for us to realize that we could no longer continue in these ungodly practices.

We marveled at how God's grace abounded, and we were able to leave this lifestyle behind with little effort. Fortunately, there were always plenty of people in line wanting to get into this assignment, so this was one more wide-open door to walk through. Step by step, we walked in the light God was giving us. Incredibly, leaving the rock culture was an easy door for us, but there would be harder challenges ahead.

The Big One

As our nights of Bible reading continued, it was not long until we made our way to the Sermon on the Mount. When I read Jesus' words about loving our enemies, I did not know what to think. I can still vividly remember leaning over on my lopsided arm pillow and reading it out loud to Tania.

"Listen to this one," I said.

> "You have heard that it was said, 'An eye for an eye and a tooth for a tooth.' But I tell you not to resist an evil person. But whoever slaps you on your right cheek, turn the other to him also. If anyone wants to sue you and take away your tunic, let him have your cloak also. And whoever compels you to go one mile, go with him two. Give to him who asks you, and from him who wants to borrow from you do not turn away.

> You have heard that it was said, 'You shall
> love your neighbor and hate your enemy.' But I
> say to you, love your enemies, bless those who
> curse you, do good to those who hate you, and
> pray for those who spitefully use you and perse-
> cute you, that you may be sons of your Father in
> heaven; for He makes His sun rise on the evil
> and on the good, and sends rain on the just and
> on the unjust. For if you love those who love
> you, what reward have you? Do not even the tax
> collectors do the same? And if you greet your
> brethren only, what do you do more than others?
> Do not even the tax collectors do so? Therefore
> you shall be perfect, just as your Father in heav-
> en is perfect" (Matthew 5:38– 48).

After reading it, I looked at Tania and said, "So what
are we supposed to do with *that?*"

"Well, it sounds pretty clear, doesn't it?" she calmly
answered.

"Yes, but we're in the Army!"

I began to ponder this passage seriously and pray. I
evaded the question for a little while by reasoning that
the theologians must have a very good explanation for
this one. Surely it had to mean more than what it literally said. I started to gather books in hopes that I would
soon find a good biblical defense for "just war" and the
role of a Christian in the military. I was sure such books
would be easy to find. After all, the church had always
believed in the idea of a "just war"—or at least that's
what I thought.

Many hours of my childhood were spent hearing he-
roic stories of brave men gallantly defending what were
portrayed as "just causes." It all seemed so right. I

could hardly imagine thinking any other way.

Childhood

Growing up, I was raised with a deep sense of patriotism. My earliest memories include family vacations to Confederate battlegrounds, battleships, and other such nationally venerable sites. I immensely enjoyed these excursions, and I remember feeling very proud of my American heritage. To consider another way of thinking on an issue such as war seemed more than just unpatriotic; it almost seemed sacrilegious. When I joined the Army I did it proudly. Serving my country was more than a service to me; it was a privilege.

My father is more "southern" than Robert E. Lee, and more "Texan" than blue bonnets. Patriotism, responsibility, and duty would define much of what motivates him. Without a doubt, "small-town Texas" runs through every vein in his body. I can still remember the time we visited the Alamo when I was about seven years old. We talked about it for months.

Getting ready for the trip, I ran around the house pretending to shoot every potential Guadalupe invader I could imagine. Once we finally arrived in San Antonio, I could hardly contain myself. Close to the "holy land," we even stayed in the nearby "Davy Crockett Motel." That first morning, I was more raring to go than a new colt.

On the "walk" to the Alamo the next morning, I tripped on a piece of uneven sidewalk and fell, cutting a deep gash on my chest just a little below my right collar bone. I laid there crying, and my father picked me up. He doctored my wound and said, imitating a tone of valor, "Well son, now you can say that you have a scar from the Alamo!" It's all kind of funny to me now, but I still have that scar, and every time I see it, I remember that day.

After making it inside the entrance of the main building, my father stopped us and directed our attention to some kind of big plaque in the floor. The best I can remember, the floor was a beige-yellowish limestone, more resembling a castle to me than what I would have imagined for a fort or mission. As tourists were shuffling in and weaving around us, we just stood there, staring down at this plaque. Then, looking up with a grin my father challenged us, pointing to the floor.

"You know what that is?"

"No," I replied. I thought to myself, "How should I know?"

Then, lifting his chin high and imitating a soldier coming to attention, my father said, "This is where Davy Crockett died. He was killed right here on this spot!"

"Wow!" My brother and I were both beyond impressed. If there was one man in history I knew all about, it was Davy Crockett. I had an old plastic record player at home that played those small 45's. My favorite record happened to be "The Ballad of Davy Crockett." That Davy Crocket record had more scratches on it than a chicken house floor, but I still managed to play it over and over and over again. Looking back, I now realize how that record must have driven my parents crazy.

Topping off the tour was the emblematic and venerable tale of the twenty-six-year-old colonel, William

Travis, who was commander of the Army of the Republic of Texas. It was the account of his famous "line in the sand." As the story goes, when it was realized that saving the Alamo was impossible, Colonel Travis called the remaining soldiers together and offered them a sobering choice.

Bravely addressing the soldiers, Col. Travis entreated, "We must die. However, our business is not to make a fruitless effort to save our lives, but to choose the manner of our death." He gave the men three choices:

- Give up and risk shame and execution
- Try to fight their way out
- Remain in the fort...resist every assault, and sell their lives as dearly as possible.[1]

Then with all the honor and gallantry of a knight from King Arthur's court, Travis slowly drew a line in the sand, crossed over the line himself, and said, "Those prepared to give their lives in freedom's cause, come over to me!"

Quickly, a young man, Tapley Holland, was the first to move. He jumped over the line and cheered, "I am ready to die for my country!" Co-commander Jim Bowie, who was injured and confined to his cot, entreated his men to carry him over the line so he could offer his life as well. All but two men crossed the line in that fateful moment—all died the next day.

Stories like that make an impact on a young boy. They certainly made an impact on me.

As I gazed up at my father, standing there like a corporal in the Foreign Legion, I realized that although by his posture he was jesting a bit, inside he was very serious. This meant something to him. Later we learned in the guided tour that when William Travis had written letters requesting help, he had valiantly signed his letters, "God and Texas, Victory or Death"—these were the axioms of my childhood.

Trip Back Home to Texas From Germany

For Christmas 1990 we flew home to Ft. Worth, Texas, to visit family and friends. During this time, I discussed some of these issues with my parents and a minister with whom I had grown up. My father took it very hard. Two times in my life I had seen my father cry. The first time was when his father died. I was seven years old at the time. The second time was the night I told him I was considering a discharge from the U.S. Army as a conscientious objector. He was sure that I was ruining my life.

Tania's family took it hard as well. Her father, Les Bokros, also had a deeply engrained sense of patriotism. At the age of nineteen, eluding gunfire, land mines, and checkpoints, he made his escape from Hungary to the United States during the Hungarian uprising of 1956. As a child he had witnessed both his father and grandfather being carried off to concentration camps. He naturally carried a great dislike for the abuses of communism and Nazism, and he greatly appreciated what he found in America.

When we talked to him, he sometimes seemed to recall childhood memories of the atrocities of warfare. At times, he even seemed to agree with us that war was wrong. He often expressed his frustration over the horrors of war and how devastating it is to the victims it claims. One time, when we finally got him talking, he related one of those wartime stories. He told us that the war years were very hard on his family. When his father was taken away to a concentration camp, life became almost impossible for his mother and his two other small siblings. They had to scrounge around for everything. Eventually, even their little farmhouse was destroyed, and the family was forced to move in with his grandmother.

He said that in some ways this wasn't so bad at first. Apparently, his grandmother's house was one of the biggest houses in the little farm town of Gyongyospata. The only problem was that its size unfortunately also made it the perfect command post for the occupying German Army.

Shortly after Les and his family moved in, the Germans took the house over as a command post and communication center for that whole region. He said that, all things considered, these German soldiers actually were very kind to him and his family.

Only about five or six years old at the time, Les actually was quite amused as he walked around and stared at all the new household additions: radios in five or six windows, wires running everywhere, a huge antiaircraft cannon on the right side of the front yard—and his favorite addition—a long, shiny, black convertible car for the commander, complete with little flags parked right outside on the front lawn! He tried to touch it once or twice, earning a chastising, "Halt! Nicht berühren!" He couldn't speak German, but figured this certainly must mean he couldn't just jump right in and try his hand at the wheel. He actually enjoyed those days, but he told us that they were to meet a sudden end.

I could see a change in his face. An intensifying, so-bering distance came over him as he told us of his last day in that house. He said that one day, while he was out in the front yard playing near the antiaircraft can-non, he looked up and saw a plane, high up in the sky. It flew over the house, came back, circled the house again, then flew away. It meant nothing to him at first. But then, suddenly, he noticed that all the German sol-diers went into a panic.

Alarms blaring, men screaming, it seemed they all knew something awful was about to happen. As his mother and sisters and grandmother were quickly tucked away into the safety of a bomb shelter, young Les thoughtlessly wandered about, hoping to get a bet-ter view of the cannon that was now in motion. All the popping, clicking, and swinging into full action was simply more than he could resist.

"Vorsicht!!"

A German soldier noticed him under the cannon. Screaming, the soldier grabbed him quite forcefully by the arm, nearly dislocating his right shoulder, and quickly threw him into the bomb shelter with the rest of his family.

"Almost immediately, I heard a sound like the world was exploding," he said.

Looking deep into his eyes, I wondered whether if I looked deeply enough, I just might be able to see what he was seeing right then in his mind. Timidly, I asked, "So then what happened?"

"I came out...and my whole world was gone. The house was completely destroyed." "You remember that cannon?" he asked. "It was blown completely to the other side of the street."

"What about the car?" I asked.

"Oh the car...I'll never forget that car. It was blown upside down. That once beautiful car was on fire and smoking—it was charred black. I remember staring at those wheels...they were still smoking as they slowly rotated around and around."

"What about the soldiers?" I probed, looking deep into his eyes.

Looking down at his feet, he said, "Oh... well, there were bodies and body parts everywhere. It was awful..."

I could tell this was hard on him. Remembering all of this, he consented, "People just don't realize what war does to children. It's cruel."

However, as if shaking himself to his original resolve, he would always insist, "But in these cases, war is necessary. Communism must be stopped."

Experiencing a childhood marred by the atrocities of communism and fascism, he could not comprehend how a position of loving one's enemies could possibly "work" to solve these types of problems.

Overall, the trip to Texas was hard. Deep inside, we ached to be able to see things the way we always had viewed them before. However, in spite of our best efforts to see things their way (or to try persuading them to see things our way), our parents, our friends, our church, and obviously our co-workers all saw the issue differently. Clearly, we were going against the flow. But as we stayed in the Word and in prayer, God's grace kept tenderly leading us onward.

As we continued to look to God for answers and direction, I started to think about another trip we had taken a year before to East Berlin. God used that trip to chip away my nationalistic paradigm. The images of that trip still continue to replay in my mind.

Chapter Two
What Changed?

Shaking Hands with a Communist

As I looked to my left, a large section of cement, covered with smears of multicolored graffiti, broke off from the top of the wall and tumbled to the ground, crashing into pieces as it hit. Cheers in Russian, English, and German seemed to ring out from every direction. Looking to my right, I saw that a group of Germans had fashioned some sort of battering ram out of an old signpost and were ramming it into the wall with all their might. Dust could be seen in the air. As it mixed in the glow of the old-fashioned security lights, it gave the night sky an eerie, orange-colored glow.

Uniformed Russian and East German soldiers were leaning through recently made holes in the wall, offering champagne and handshakes as they shouted and sang of peace and brotherhood. It seemed completely dreamlike to me standing there just a few yards away from the infamous "Checkpoint Charlie." I was witnessing the Berlin wall literally being torn down to the ground by hand.

What made the experience even more remarkable to me was that barely a year earlier I had walked through that same checkpoint. Only the setting had been completely different. In compliance with the strict mandate that I be in full uniform, I had made my way through an intimidating exhibition of surveillance cameras, concertina wire, and machine gun toting wall guards. Once on the Eastern side, a man had even spit down at my feet as I walked by in my polished military shoes.

I had enjoyed my trip to the Eastern side, but I remember being puzzled that in East Berlin, the quality of life differed quite notably just on the other side of this man-made partition. But now, right before my eyes, that very partition was coming down. Caught up in the excitement of it all, my wife and I and another couple from the Army band, Rick and Dawn Shirley, joined in taking potshots at the wall to see if we could tear a little bit down. As I stood there taking it all in, I pondered the contrast between the two trips to Berlin. The question that pummeled my mind was this—*what changed?*

This staggering question continued to dominate my thoughts as I made my way back home. In those days, travel between West Germany and Berlin required driving a long and lonely stretch of about 110 miles of fenced off, nearly ghost town-looking freeway. West Berlin sat like an island in the middle of communist East Germany. Although the Berlin wall now was coming down, it was a few years before the East and West actually united. A thoroughfare linked the East with the West through a series of fortified NATO and communist checkpoints.

Arriving at the first checkpoint in Helmstedt, we had undergone a series of briefings. The military guards had warned us not to stop, slow down, sightsee, or even break down on the three-hour trip through East Germany. They had even given us a folder with pictures of our exit signs and papers containing various Russian and German phrases to ward off possible undesirable encounters. We were instructed not to even roll down our windows or speak to anyone, but to hold up an appropriate sign in our car window should we need help for any reason. We also had needed to complete a series of security briefings back home before being granted permission to visit. We were fully aware of the strict regulations we would be expected to observe.

The ride into East Germany was uneventful. We

drove in without a hitch. The only notable thing was that while we were sailing in on the Eastbound side, lines of cars were bumper to bumper in the Westbound lanes, as hundreds of barely operable Russian cars made their newly legalized exodus from the East. I couldn't help but wonder if this traffic jam would be awaiting us on our way out.

Traffic, however, would prove to be the least of our problems. Pushing our trip to the limit, we didn't head back to the West until late at night. That probably would have been okay if it hadn't started to snow heavily. As we checked out of our hotel and headed to the first checkpoint to leave East Berlin, the snow was really coming down. Having been raised in Texas, I had little experience with snow. It was very intimidating to me. I recommended to our group that we stay one more night in the hotel. Unfortunately, however, I wasn't driving.

As providence would have it, Russell, a young Army band member from Michigan, had driven us to Berlin, so we were completely at his mercy for the ride home. Tania and I tried to encourage ourselves that Russell was born and raised in Michigan, so he should be used to driving in such conditions. Besides that, he surely seemed confident, albeit young and inexperienced. He insisted that he was more than competent to drive at top speeds in heavy snowfall as he always had done before in Michigan.

As we plowed our way through the heavy snow on the way home, feeling little slips here and there, we tried to hold our tongues and give poor Russell a chance to prove himself. But alas, we could take it no longer! We started out gently, "Russell, could you please slow it down just a bit?"

Finally, we found ourselves somewhat outraged, "Russell, we may be from Texas, but if you don't slow down, you're going to kill us! This can't be safe!"

It seemed the more Tania and I protested from the back seat, the faster and more recklessly young Russell drove. All the while, he continually insisted that, being from Michigan, he was well accustomed to driving in far worse conditions than these. I started to really question how this was all going to work out.

By the time we neared the first checkpoint of the one hundred and ten-mile fenced-off road to the West, the snow was coming down in sheets. However, it seemed that it just *might* be somewhat manageable. So, lacking the needed experience and discernment to make a proper judgment call in the situation, we decided to head out on the long crossing. Inevitably, it wasn't far down the road until the snowfall really started to get worse. The flakes poured down like showers of silver dollars. As we continued on, the situation became down-right frightening, as the wind picked up and created moments of pure white-out.

We all knew that once we passed that first checkpoint, there was no place to stop, pull over, or turn around. Our friends Rick and Dawn Shirley were in the car ahead of us, and we tried desperately to keep each other in view. However, the storm steadily continued to worsen, and visibility was quickly diminishing. My friend kept driving so fast that the car began sliding more and more.

"This is ridiculous!" I protested, "You have got to slow down!"

"Ah, this is nothing!" he barked back. "You should

see the snow in Michigan!"

Slip—Crash—Fluff!

The inevitable finally happened, as we lost control and crashed into a snow bank. After trying to pull ourselves out and start the car, we eventually gave up.

We sat there—numb—in silence.

There we were...stuck in the snow... in the middle of a blizzard...in a communist country...in between checkpoints…in the middle of the night...in a broken down car…in a place where we were instructed not to speak to anyone, but to use signs that might fit our particular calamity to communicate! On top of it all, we would now be absent from work the next day without proper permission (AWOL)!

There was no sense blaming anyone. We immediately started to think about survival. Fortunately, by the divine mercy of God, there were four of us in the car, and we each had purchased big fluffy blankets from the Eastern side as souvenirs! So, we bundled up and prayed that when Rick and Dawn reached the checkpoint and noticed that we never made it over, they would send for help. It proved to be one long, cold, restless night.

As the sun slowly began to creep its way up over the horizon, we noticed that the snow had now stopped and we sat there completely covered in several inches of snow.

Then it happened...the "enemy" started to come over to us. The only puzzling thing was that they weren't acting much like enemies. These "enemies" were simply East Germans who had spotted us there stranded in the snow. They felt compassion for us and offered to help.

Afraid of the political ramifications of talking to "communists," we tried to remain good American soldiers and rejected their help. I still can vividly remember one of them standing there at the window, offering us a steaming hot thermos of coffee. It looked so good! But with all the programming and propaganda we had received on espionage and the communist threat, we couldn't help but wonder if he might be a spy. So we rejected his kindness. This all seems rather silly now.

Eventually, a wrecking truck came by and took us back to Berlin. As we were there going through the difficulty of proving why we were back in Berlin, I thought about how friendly the face of my enemy was. I couldn't get the image of that steaming hot thermos of coffee out of my mind. I had played up the communists in my mind to be monsters. But my enemy had offered me a drink, and as it says in the end of Romans 12, he had "heaped burning coals upon my head."

Back Home

Thinking about all of this when I got home, it really bothered me that only a month before I could have been called on to shoot these men. But now, due to a few political changes, they were considered my allies. The obvious fact was that, in reality, nothing had changed. The only change that had taken place was that a few days before, a small group of global leaders had gotten together, made a decision, and suddenly my enemy had become my friend. This bothered me.

I wondered how God looks at these man-made walls. And then I wondered how God wanted *me* to look at them. Should my love for others await the order of human authority? Or has an even higher authority already called a truce and broken down these walls? Later, as I began to study the Bible, I realized that in Christ, those walls had already been torn down two thousand years ago.

Christ Has Broken Down the Wall of Partition

In the Old Testament era, The Hebrews were a major source of nationalistic contention to the world around them. In the time of King David, Solomon, and the subsequent kings, even the very geographic area of the nation was considered "God's country." National pride and elitism was not the result of some big egos; it was a historical and biblical fact. But when Christ came, God in His mercy expanded His kingdom to include all who by faith believe on His Son. The fulfillment of all the promises, covenants, blessings, and even the genealogical lineage of the chosen people all came to reside in the person of Jesus Christ. When I gave my life to Christ, I became a partaker of all these covenantal blessings and promises of God.

Ever since the time of Christ, every person, nation, and tribe is offered citizenship in God's kingdom by coming into it through His Son Jesus Christ. What I came to understand was that although Christians have been scattered throughout hundreds of countries and thousands of years, in Christ, these nationalistic dividing walls all have been taken down. This means that as citizens of this Christian kingdom, I live here in my earthly kingdom as a stranger and pilgrim. My true citizenship and belonging are in Christ.

To the church at Ephesus, the Apostle Paul wrote, "For He Himself is our peace, who has made both one, and has broken down the middle wall of separation, having abolished in His flesh the enmity, that is, the law of commandments contained in ordinances, so as to create in Himself one new man from the two, thus making peace, and that He might reconcile them both to God in one body through the cross, thereby putting to death the enmity" (Ephesians 2:14–16).

To the church at Colossi, Paul wrote that we "have put on the new man who is renewed in knowledge according to the image of Him who created him, where there is neither Greek nor Jew, circumcised nor uncircumcised, barbarian, Scythian, slave nor free, but Christ is all and in all" (Colossians 3:10–11). This liberating and empowering truth broke down my national and political walls. I found it a profound truth that all who are in Christ exist as God's "chosen people," no matter which natural country they come from.

As I pondered this truth about the Kingdom of God, my entire world changed. It was not that I became rebellious or defiant of my American citizenship. Rather, I was overcome by an even greater and more encompassing identity. My entrenched sense of patriotism and nationalistic pride began to falter under the revelation of this vast kingdom. I marveled that throughout centuries of time, this kingdom of God has continued to march forward. Empire after empire has come and gone; nations have been raised, and nations have fallen, but this Kingdom of God has remained. The Medes,

Persians, Greeks, and Romans all have died out. The pride and schemes of powerful leaders such as Alexander the Great, Attila the Hun, Genghis Khan, Caesar Augustus, Napoleon, Mussolini, Hitler, and even Stalin have amounted to nothing more than confusion and needless bloodshed.

Old Testament Prophesy

More than 700 years before the New Testament era, the prophet Isaiah spoke about the triumphant, eternal nature of the Kingdom of God. He wrote:

> "For every battle of the warrior is with confused noise, and garments rolled in blood; but this shall be with burning and fuel of fire. For unto us a child is born, unto us a son is given: and the government shall be upon his shoulder: and his name shall be called Wonderful, Counsellor, The mighty God, The everlasting Father, The Prince of Peace. Of the increase of his government and peace there shall be no end" (Isaiah 9:5–7).

This newfound realization wasn't easy for me. In a way, I felt I was losing all that had been dear to me. All these changes were causing me to realize that deep within me, there was a strong need for acceptance and belonging. Losing my national, political, and even familial identity was threatening to unravel my very moral fabric. Indeed, citizenship was a coveted privilege to me. Especially as a soldier, I felt I was now doing my part to fight to maintain it. There was no doubt that these emotions ran deep.

But a question I began to ask myself was, "Where

should I put these feelings?" For a while I felt that these emotions were part of the old man, a carnal desire that needed to be put away. But as I continued to study and pray, I realized that God had put this drive within me for a reason; it merely needed to be redirected.

As the writer of Hebrews said, "By faith Abraham, when he was called to go out into a place which he should after receive for an inheritance, obeyed; and he went out, not knowing whither he went. By faith he sojourned in the land of promise, as in a strange country, dwelling in tabernacles with Isaac and Jacob, the heirs with him of the same promise: *For he looked for a city* which hath foundations, whose builder and maker is God" (Hebrews 11:8–10).

Unfortunately, for most of my life the ability to express this natural quest for belonging existed only in the sense of a worldly patriotism for partisan causes. In the end, this type of patriotism was divisive and egocentric. Often accompanying this partisan-type spirit was the strange habit I had of showing my loyalty to my side by hating my opponents. When there really was nothing genuine to give allegiance to, it became easiest simply to despise everything that didn't agree with me. I realized that this type of partisanship could never fill the void that God wanted to fill in my heart. Emptiness and controversy had always been the proven result. As I considered humanity on the larger scale, it became obvious that patriotism such as this had fueled disputes and fights for thousands of years, ranging anywhere from high school rivalries to nuclear wars.

I became convinced that God did not put this drive in me for the sake of egocentrism or contention. He put it in me to motivate me to seek His Kingdom, where He alone reigns as King.

Speaking of this God-given desire, the writer of Hebrews goes on to say that Abraham and the ancient people of faith also sought for this belonging and resting place in God's Kingdom saying; "For those who say such things declare plainly that they seek a homeland. And truly if they had called to mind that country from which they had come out, they would have had opportunity to return. But now they desire a better, that is, a heavenly country. Therefore God is not ashamed to be called their God, for He has prepared a city for them" (Hebrews 11:14–16).

Putting It Together

Now that I was reading the Bible and asking questions, I thought back on that Berlin trip. The fall of the Berlin wall planted seeds that opened my eyes to many of these truths.

But while I pondered the aspects of these two kingdoms, more questions arose in my mind. Taking it further as I considered history, I pondered, "How has the church justified all the wars throughout the centuries?" Countless holy wars, crusades, and endless "just" causes all seemed to be conflicting with the plain truth of God's Word—"Love your enemies."

I was not comfortable just to let this matter go, so I went on a search to find the arguments for a "just war." I started to look at church history to see how the church dealt with all this. I wanted to see exactly where the Just War Theory originated, and I was shocked with what I found.

Chapter Three
Something Went Terribly Wrong

Belt buckle for Nazi soldiers in WWII   which proclaimed

"God With Us"

"It is now full time for the emperor to provide for the safety of the Catholic church, and prevent those rash men from terrifying the people, whom they cannot seduce."[1]

Such were the fatal words decreed at a church council held at Carthage in the year 404. Three bishops presided, Alypius, Fortunatus, and the well-known bishop whom history has called "Saint Augustine." It was during this council that Augustine's legendary Just War Theory had its formal debut.

As I studied this Just War Theory, I didn't like what I found. Its origin goes back to a series of debates that Augustine had with several theological opponents. I read that after years of theological debate, Augustine had begun to lose confidence in his power of verbal persuasion. His chief opponents at the time, the Donatists, had broken away from the main body of the "catholic" church almost a century before. Many had tried to convince them to rejoin the Catholics, but none had succeeded. These Donatists were zealous and persuasive. Worst of all, they were growing in number.[2] But now, at this council in Carthage, North Africa, the church decided that these "heretics" must be stopped— regardless of the means used. The council asked the Roman government to intervene by reinstating laws that the pagan Romans had written originally against Christians many decades before.

The Roman emperor was already under great pressure. During this time a group of invaders from eastern Germany known as the Visigoths, had crossed over the borders of the Roman Empire, looting cities as they came. Eventually, they made their way to the main cities, and by A.D. 410, the city of Rome was finally taken. During that dreadful siege, many citizens starved to death, and it is reported that some even succumbed to acts of cannibalism. With the obvious pressures from the outside, domestic troubles could not be tolerated. Internal division from the rapidly growing Christian religion was the last thing the emperor wanted. With such an invitation, the state gladly stepped in to "fix" the church's problem. The Emperor eventually proclaimed:

> "We decree that the Donatists and the heretics, who until now have been spared by the patience of Our Clemency, shall be severely punished by legal authority, so that by this Our manifest order, they shall recognize that they are detestable and have no power of entering into contracts of any kind, but they shall be branded with perpetual infamy and separated from honorable gatherings and from public assemblies. Those places in which the dire superstition has been preserved until now shall surely be joined to the venerable Catholic church, and thus their bishops and priests, that is, all their prelates and ministers shall likewise be despoiled of all their property and shall be sent into exile to separate islands and provinces."[3]

I was staggered...what a switch! The persecuted Christians had now become the persecutors!

The abuse and persecution that followed was dreadful. Historian Edward Gibbon reports that at this time, 300 bishops, with many thousands of deacons and other ministers, were torn from their churches, stripped of their church possessions, and banished to remote islands. If the ministers decided to stay, they were put under strict laws regulating every part of their lives. Furthermore, all the members of their churches—both in the cities and in the country—were deprived of the rights given to other Roman citizens. Naturally, worship or any other type of religious gathering was completely forbidden to the Donatists. Large fines of gold and silver were copiously charged. Resistors were put into prison, and eventually, if they would not repent, were killed.

The Donatists, in a plea for mercy, challenged Augustine, saying that he was making martyrs out of their bishops and elders. They warned him that God would require him to give an account for their blood on the Day of Judgment. To this, Augustine defiantly replied, "I know nothing about your martyrs. Martyrs! Martyrs to the devil. There are no martyrs out of the church. Beside, it was their obstinacy; they killed themselves."[4]

Augustine's Theology

Entangled within Augustine's view of a "Just War" were his views of purgatory and eternal judgment. He felt that since the Donatists actually were misguided "Christians," torturing them in this life actually could be viewed as an act of mercy. Even if they were killed, he reasoned, it would be to their eternal good.[5] Looking for support from a passage of scripture customarily used for evangelism, Augustine gave a novel interpretation to Jesus' words in Luke 15 about "compelling" people into God's kingdom.

Augustine reasoned,

> "It is indeed better that men should be brought
> to serve God by instruction than by fear of
> punishment or by pain. But because the former
> means are better, the latter must not therefore be
> neglected…Many must often be brought back to
> their Lord, like wicked servants, by the rod of
> temporal suffering, before they attain the
> highest grade of religious development…The
> Lord himself orders that the guests be first
> invited, then compelled, to his great supper."[6]

The Seed Grew

A contemporary of Augustine named Cyril was ordained in A.D. 412 as the Bishop of Alexandria. With
the thought of defending God and purifying the church,
Cyril took the ideas of the Just War Theory and ran
with them. Under his influence things quickly went
from bad to worse. Like Augustine, he took a strong
stand against the Donatists. But he also led attacks on
other groups of Christians such as the Novationists.

The Novationists were a zealous group of Christians
who also had left the Catholic church a century earlier,
due to growing worldliness in the church. Cyril and his
monks led persecuting campaigns against both the Donatists and the Novationists. But he did not stop with
Christians. He also led attacks against synagogues and
burned down whole libraries, killing heretics, Jews, and
any pagan that came in his way.

One of the most graphic examples of the appalling
nature of the times was a hideous scene that occurred
when a band of Cyril's men met a famous pagan philos-

opher named Hypatia as she drove by in her carriage. The men recognized her, stopped the chariot, and then dragged her from her seat. Demonstrating nothing but barbarous savagery, the group proceeded to strip her flesh from her bones with sharpened sea shells while she was still alive. After she finally died, the zealous group carried pieces of her body around through the streets and eventually threw them into a fire along with her pagan books.

Certainly, all would agree that something had gone terribly wrong. However, given the nature of the times, it all seemed justifiable—even rational! In this case, no one was even punished for the murder. Cyril went on to persuade the emperor, Theodosius II, to banish all remaining Jews from Alexandria, and to increase the persecution of pagan priests. By A.D. 416, the church and state had grown so close together that Christians not only were joining the military, but mass baptisms also were conducted, and anyone who would not convert to Christianity was kicked out of the Army!

Unfortunately, this venomous ideology did not stop with Cyril. Throughout the centuries, other church leaders have leaned on Augustine's logic to sanctify their own "just" causes. It was not hard to see that throughout history, haunting the church like a generational curse, Augustine's Just War Theory has continued to defile the church by twisting the simple words of Jesus. Church historian, F. W. Farrar, considering the ramifications of Augustine's theology, makes a candid confession:

> "Augustine must bear the fatal charge of being the first as well as one of the ablest defenders of the frightful cause of persecution and intolerance. He

was the first to misuse the words "*Compel Them To Come In.*" He was the first and ablest asserter of the principle that led to the Albigensian crusades, Spanish armadas, Netherlands' butcheries, St Bartholomew massacres, the accursed infamies of the Inquisition, the vile espionage, the hideous balefires of Seville and Smithfield, the racks, the gibbets, the thumbscrews, the subterranean torture-chambers...

It is mainly because of his later intolerance that the influence of Augustine falls like a dark shadow across the centuries. It is thus that [centuries of brutal persecutors] can look up to him as an author-izer of their enormities, and quote his sentences to defend some of the vilest crimes which ever caused men to look with horror on the religion of Christ and the church of God."[7]

Most Christians today would agree that these historical accounts are both grotesque and inexcusable. We scratch our heads in bewilderment as we ponder how professing Christians could have ever come to such a point. Reading of the accounts surrounding the church during these times of debate and unrest sobered me.

The Crusades

The Crusades are another poignant example of the dangers lurking in a "just war" theology. Today, most Christians see the Crusades as a big mistake, both politically and spiritually. As obviously wrong as these wars seem to us now, it is instructive for us to see how justifiable they looked to their perpetrators at the time. In an epic, world-changing speech, Pope Urban II called on all of heaven and earth to aid in his initiation of the first crusade. In his speech, he exclaimed that the Muslim people had committed great atrocities against the pilgrims to the Holy Land, and postulated what that meant to the church everywhere if the Muslims were not stopped. So sure was he in his campaign that he even promised eternal salvation to all who fought and died for this cause.

These are the words taken directly from that speech, which started the first Crusade:

> "On this account I, or rather the Lord, beseech you as Christ's heralds to publish this every-where and to persuade all people of whatever rank, foot-soldiers and knights, poor and rich, to carry aid promptly to those Christians and to de-stroy that vile race from the lands of our friends. I say this to those who are present; it is meant also for those who are absent. Moreover, Christ commands it. All who die by the way, whether by land or by sea, or in battle against the pagans, shall have immediate remission of sins. This I grant them through the power of God with which I am invested."[8]

This battle cry greatly moved the crowd to action. It is reported that in a shout of triumph the crowd roared and chanted with one voice, "It is the will of God! It is the will of God!"[9]

Nazi Germany

In World War II Germany, the Nazis demonstrated a spirit much like the religious enthusiasm of the former Crusaders. The fanatical dedication, ethnocentric rhetoric, and symbolism of Nazi Germany were frightfully similar to those of the Holy Roman Empire during the time of the Crusades. Revival-like fervor, flashing swastikas, and battle cries inspired the German people to terrorize the entire Western world. Yet, throughout all the bloodshed and terror, each benighted Nazi soldier believed that the German cause was just and even blessed of God. A look back at war memorabilia from this era plainly reveals this fact. Blazoned right across such items as cigarette lighters, trinket boxes, and every soldier's belt buckle was their presumptuous banner "Gott Mit Uns" (God with us).

When in Germany, Tania and I had the opportunity to visit with some people who were alive during the Nazi era. One elderly couple we talked to, Hans Jacob and Renata, were older than 70 years when we met them. Hans was a young man during World War II. I asked him, "How did it happen? How did the majority of the church just go along with it? How did it seem reasonable?" He looked at me soberly and said, "It's hard to explain...it just swept over us like a spirit."

Me

As I first pondered these displays of pride and egocentrism that I read about from these old wars, I told myself that they were merely old-fashioned and archaic attitudes out of place in the modern world. However, as I thought longer about it, I had to admit to myself that these attitudes were a whole lot closer than I cared to believe. I found that these same root motives and prejudices actually were lurking deep down in my own heart.

Thinking back to my basic training experiences, I recalled a gruesome exercise that could possibly have made even some of the Crusaders envious. Standing in an open field with 500 vigorous, enthused young men, we were ordered to raise our M-16 machine guns high into the air and scream at the top of our lungs various morbid cadences. I vividly remember the faces of these men surrounding me. They were brutal and serious. Veins popping, cheeks puffing, and spit and froth flying, we all were screaming with everything we had in us.

In one of these cadences, I recalled how the drill sergeant stood in front of us, shouted out a few intimidating expletives, and then bellowed out the chilling cry:

—WHAT MAKES THE GRASS GROW? —

To this, we were to reply as loud as we could scream...

— "BLOOD, BLOOD, BLOOD! –BLOOD MAKES THE GRASS GROW!" —

Then while thrusting our machine guns equipped with bayonets up and down into the air, as if we were impaling the sky, we began to scream and chant rhythmically the words,

— "KILL, KILL, WITH COLD BLUE STEEL—KILL, KILL, WITH COLD BLUE STEEL—KILL, KILL, WITH COLD BLUE STEEL!" —

Looking back, I'm not quite sure what we all were

thinking. It felt surreal—almost humorous—much more like a bunch of little boys playing army than anything really serious. Afterward, we all just went on to the chapel or lunch without much thought of the drill. After thinking about it more, however, I realized the whole thing wasn't funny at all. What we were doing was not make believe—it was very real. Those "toys" we had in our hands fired real bullets that killed real people.

But even more serious than this, I distinctly remember that even when I did soberly reflect about actually using my weapon to kill someone, I somehow felt completely rational about it all. Much like the Nazis or the Crusaders, I too reasoned that we were the civilized and "right" ones. I felt that somehow all this was okay, and that God was "with us" and blessing us. Just like the enraged Roman soldiers running to the papal battle cry, I was convinced that my cause was just! Later, I felt convicted that I needed to repent of this root of evil in my heart.

The more I read, the more I asked questions; the more I asked questions, the more uneasy I became. I was beginning to accept the words of Jesus more and more. But for a time, it just seemed that the more I accepted the words of Jesus, the more questions I found myself asking. Perhaps one of my biggest questions was what to do with the Old Testament wars. If I was to receive the *entire* Bible as the Word of God, then how could I explain the paradox of God clearly calling for war in the Old Testament, and Jesus clearly forbidding war in the New Testament?

Chapter Four
The God of the Bible

My locker in the Army—with a new sign

One of the most perplexing questions I found myself facing was what to do with all of the Old Testament wars. As I read some of the books and listened to some of the arguments, I felt divided. Early in my reading, it seemed to me that most of the conservative writers were not consistent or even honest with the New Testament. On the other hand, as I began to read writers from the liberal camp, it seemed that many of their arguments were not honest with the Old Testament.

In some of the newer liberal books, God was displayed as a "nonviolent" deity who would never condemn or hurt anyone. The writers seemed to imply that God really doesn't punish people, and He certainly would never sentence someone to Hell for eternity. Often, Jesus was represented as a person who came to proclaim universal, nonviolent, nonjudgmental, all-accepting salvation for everyone. All the violent acts in the Old Testament were summed up as having been outside the divine will of God. They were merely the result of man "messing things up," so to speak.

Following the lead of the liberals, I attempted to read the Old Testament in such a way that I too could explain away each act of violence or war as merely a mistake on man's part, and not God's perfect will. I did find a few good examples, such as the statement, "thou shall not kill" from the Old Testament Law. Or the story about Abraham avoiding conflicts over the water wells. There was even the story about the revivals under Jehoshaphat, in which God said, "Ye shall not need to fight in this battle: set yourselves, stand ye still, and see the salvation of the LORD with you" (2 Chronicles 20:17).

However, I eventually realized that my liberal glasses were flawed. When I was completely honest with myself, I felt that there simply was no way, even in my most generous rendering, that I could excuse every act of war and violence in the Old Testament as merely "man's mistakes." Even the command "thou shall not kill" from the Ten Commandments was clearly a reference dealing specifically with unlawful murder. To my dismay, I found that the very Old Testament law that established "thou shall not kill" also established "an eye for an eye and a tooth for a tooth!" I had to admit that all throughout the Old Testament, wars and battles were actually called for by a direct command of God.

No, I did not find in the Old Testament a "pacifist" God at all! Quite the contrary, I found just the opposite. I found that the Scriptures portray God as a warrior. As it says in Exodus, "The LORD is a man of war: the LORD is his name" (Exodus 15:3). These passages challenged me, but I needed to accept this truth, as much as any other, if I were to understand truly the God of the Scriptures.

Holy, Holy, Holy

Although it certainly is true that God is represented as immeasurably gracious, merciful, and forgiving, He also is revealed to us as being holy. That's a funny word today. In its most simple translation, the word means separate, or rather, "set apart"—not aloof, irritated, or even sanctimonious, but separate. Separate in that God is completely above and beyond humans in morality, justice, righteousness, and love.

One of the few glimpses of God given in the Bible is from the prophet Isaiah when he received a vision of Heaven. When Isaiah came face to face with the holiness of God, it changed his life.

> "I saw the Lord sitting on a throne, high and lifted up, and the train of His robe filled the temple. Above it stood seraphim; each one had six wings: with two he covered his face, with two he covered his feet, and with two he flew. And one cried to another and said:
> 'Holy, holy, holy is the LORD of hosts; The whole earth is full of His glory!' And the posts of the door were shaken by the voice of him who cried out, and the house was filled with smoke. So I said: 'Woe is me, for I am undone! Because I am a man of unclean lips, And I dwell in the midst of a people of unclean lips; For my eyes have seen the King, The LORD of hosts.'"[1]

I felt that this understanding of the Old Testament was essential if I was going to understand the real God of the Bible.

R. C. Sproul, commenting on this passage wrote, "The Bible says that God is holy, holy, holy. Not that He is merely holy, or even holy, holy. He is holy, holy, holy. The Bible never says that God is love, love, love, or mercy, mercy, mercy, or wrath, wrath, wrath, or justice, justice, justice. It does say that He is holy, holy, holy, the whole earth is full of His glory."[2]

This holiness is morally pure; there is no trace of defilement. As I was beginning to consider the God of the Old Testament, I often identified with the feelings of Isaiah: "Woe is me! for I am undone because I am a man of unclean lips, and I dwell in the midst of a people of unclean lips."[3]

As I attempted to grasp the holiness of God, I suddenly was gripped with the reality that everything about me was deficient: my speech, my life, and even my own people group. And unlike us, God does not have to try to "be good" or "keep the Law" as we do. The Law flows from His very essence. God is perfect, noncompromising, nonchanging, and just. This is the God I saw revealed in the Old Testament.

Moses

One of the most impressive accounts of God revealing Himself describes what happened shortly after He gave the Old Testament Law to Moses. Pleading with God, Moses cried, "Please, show me Your glory."[4] Moses began to beg God to show him more completely who He was. The burning bush, the pillar of fire, and a cloud of smoke were not enough. Moses wanted even closer intimacy and begged God to show him all of His Glory. God explained that He could not completely grant Moses his request because it would kill him. However, God permitted Moses to see a portion of His glory as He went behind a rock. God said, "So it shall be, while My glory passes by, that I will put you in the cleft of the rock, and will cover you with My hand while I pass by."[5]

Could you imagine having been there when this happened? I wonder how I would have recorded what happened. The way Moses recorded this for us in Exodus is somewhat peculiar. Instead of describing God's physical appearance, Moses described God by

His attributes, or rather in definitions that express His very nature or essence:

> "And the LORD descended in the cloud, and stood with him there, and proclaimed the name of the LORD. And the LORD passed by before him, and proclaimed, The LORD, The LORD God, merciful and gracious, longsuffering, and abundant in goodness and truth, Keeping mercy for thousands, forgiving iniquity and transgression and sin."

What a beautiful picture of God's mercy. I am eternally grateful for the compassion of God displayed there before Moses. However, as beautiful as this is, it is only half the picture. Moses went on to reveal even more about God's nature:

> "And that will by no means clear the guilty; visiting the iniquity of the fathers upon the children, and upon the children's children, unto the third and to the fourth generation."[6]

That phrase in the middle of verse seven still gets me: "and that will by no means clear the guilty." What Moses is saying here about God's character is that God will not just overlook sin. If a law of God is broken, then it must be punished. In other words, God will not just say, "Ah, that's all right...Go on, just forget about it...It's okay."

This passage showed me that sin in my life is serious to God. I can't just ignore it. I must deal with it. To be honest, pondering this truth still makes me tremble. But it also makes me rejoice when I consider what abundant grace and forgiveness have come to us through Jesus

Christ. Jesus made the provision for that guilt finally to
be taken away and cleared.

Going on with Moses, God revealed yet another
attribute of His nature with an even more curious description—"For the LORD, whose name is Jealous, is a
jealous God."[7]

"Jealous"—what a name! This is the God of the Old
Testament. That didn't sound like the all-inclusive God
I had recently been reading about. It sounded closer to
the idea that "God is a warrior."

Jesus

Now I had to come to terms with who God is in the
New Testament, and at times this seemed a great paradox. If Jesus is "the express image" of God,[8] then why
didn't He teach the same thing in the New Testament as
in the Old? How could I explain the life example and
teaching of Christ? Jesus' radical call to nonresistance,
loving our enemies, and even doing good to those who
mistreat us seemed diametrically to contradict the idea
of God being a warrior. If God in the Old Testament
said, "an eye for eye and a tooth for a tooth,"[9] then how
could Jesus now say, "Ye have heard that it hath been
said, An eye for an eye, and a tooth for a tooth: But I
say unto you, That ye resist not evil: but whosoever
shall smite thee on thy right cheek, turn to him the
other."[10] How could I reconcile the differences?

God Cannot Change

I began to understand that the change from the Old to
the New Testament was not a change in the nature or

character of God, but a change in how we serve God, and ultimately, how we live in His Kingdom. The heart of God has never changed. As a matter of fact, God *cannot* change. Scripture tells us that there is not even the slightest hint of the ability to change within the nature of God, "with whom there is no variation or shadow of turning."[11]

In the New Covenant, God is just as holy and zealous to establish His Kingdom as He ever was. He also is just as serious about our lives being dedicated to Him alone as He was in the Old Testament. In this sense, you could still call His name "Jealous." Making "peace" is not an end unto itself; it is not God's final goal. As a matter of fact, speaking of what radical devotion to Him would produce in relationships, Jesus said:

> "Do not think that I came to bring peace on earth. I did not come to bring peace but a sword. For I have come to 'set a man against his father, a daughter against her mother, and a daughter-in-law against her mother-in-law'; and 'a man's enemies will be those of his own household'. He who loves father or mother more than Me is not worthy of Me. And he who loves son or daughter more than Me is not worthy of Me."[12]

Change

All that said, the changes that Jesus made when He came to earth were momentous, even revolutionary. The war for the souls of men still rages on. What changed was *how* we go to war. As I read through the Sermon on the Mount, it became clear to me that Jesus was incontestably making significant changes in life-style, worship, and behaviors. Six times in the beginning of the Sermon on the Mount, Jesus begins His radical changes with "Ye have heard that it hath been said," or "Ye have heard that it was said by them of old time." Dismissing the old as if it were already centuries expired, Jesus initiates His changes with the daring manifesto, "But I say unto you...." This is significant.

It is significant for two reasons. First, it is significant for the very fact that a change of this magnitude was even made in the first place. I felt that recognition of this fact was the only way to be honest with harmonizing the two Testaments. Just like the changes made in dealing with temple worship and salvation, these changes in lifestyle, devotion, and even war were obviously substantial. The writer of Hebrews said:

> "For if that first covenant had been faultless, then no place would have been sought for a second. Because finding fault with them, He says: 'Behold, the days are coming, says the LORD, when I will make a new covenant with the house of Israel and with the house of Judah'... In that He says, 'A new covenant', He has made the first obsolete. Now what is becoming obsolete and growing old is ready to vanish away."[13]

This does not make the Old Testament irrelevant. Again, the heart of God has never changed. Understanding God's heart can help guide our zeal and passion. What has changed is the means by which God's will is to be accomplished and manifested.

The Authority of Jesus

The second significant thing to note is *who* was making the change. Only Jesus had the authority to make such unquestionable changes. No prophet or disciple had the authority to make such changes, not even John the Baptist.

No one in history before or afterward had authority to make changes as Jesus did. The last verse in Jesus' Sermon on the Mount reveals the way people perceived His teachings, "And so it was, when Jesus had ended these sayings, that the people were astonished at His teaching, for He taught them as one having authority, and not as the scribes."[14]

So now it was all becoming more clear to me. To understand the question, "How do we deal with the Old Testament," I first realized that the nature of God has not and cannot change. God is still a warrior. On the other hand, I also came to terms with the fact that the way we "fight" the battle in the new covenant has undergone a complete metamorphosis.

Examples of the New Battle Plan

Not only did Jesus give these teachings to us explicitly, He also practiced them as a living demonstration of His new way. Once, when Jesus and His disciples were planning to pass though the village of the Samaritans, noticing that they were just passing through, the Samaritans conspired to stop them by not allowing them to enter.

James and John, remembering the Old Testament way that Elijah had dealt with a challenge similar to this, asked Jesus if they could call down fire from heaven and annihilate them. "'Lord, do You want us to command fire to come down from heaven and consume them, just as Elijah did'? But He turned and rebuked them, and said, 'You do not know what manner of spirit you are of. For the Son of Man did not come to destroy men's lives but to save them'. And they went to another village."[15] Jesus demonstrated that the New Testament battle plan was for salvation, not destruction.

We see another conspicuous example when Jesus was being apprehended in the Garden of Gethsemane right before His crucifixion. This opportunity afforded a very pointed object lesson. Not long before Jesus' abduction in the garden, Jesus had given the apostles a missionary charge significantly different from the first one. This one was going to be for the long haul. In the first commission Jesus had told them to take nothing, no money or even a change of clothes. But now Jesus, anticipating a longer journey, instructed them to pack several things: "And He said to them, 'When I sent you without money bag, knapsack, and sandals, did you lack anything'? So they said, 'Nothing'. Then He said to them, 'But now, he who has a money bag, let him take it, and likewise a knapsack.'"[16]

One of the things Jesus told them to pack along with the other provisions was a "sword" saying, "and he who has no sword, let him sell his garment and buy one."[17]

After the instructions, the apostles found two swords and said, "'Lord, look, here are two swords.' And He said to them, 'It is enough.'"[18]

People argue about the size of these swords. Exactly how big these swords were is a debate that will never be answered. Regardless of their size, the important point of the object lesson is that Peter was trying to use this thing as a weapon to defend Jesus. When the guards came to take Jesus, the disciples asked Him, "Lord, shall we strike with the sword?"[19]

Without waiting for an answer, Peter reared up and hacked off the ear of Malchus, who was a servant of the High Priest. Jesus then reached down, picked up Malchus' ear, miraculously reattached it, and made the proclamation: "Put up again thy sword into his place: for all they that take the sword shall perish with the sword."[20]

Significant words, significant command, and a notably significant change. That's not the way they did it in the Old Testament! This clearly was a change in the battle plan. Furthermore, Jesus' pronouncement on those who "live by the sword" is weighty, to say the least.

There is an interesting quote from way back in the early church that speaks of what resulted from this decree. Tertullian, an early Christian, writing as early as A.D. 190 asked concerning this verse:

> "How will a Christian man participate in war? In fact, how will he serve even in peace without a sword? For the Lord has taken the sword away. It is also true that soldiers came to John the Baptist and received the instructions for their conduct. It is true also that a centurion believed. Nevertheless, the Lord afterward, in disarming Peter, disarmed every soldier."[21]

To understand finally the God of the Old Testament was to understand my purpose in life as I never had before. I now understood that God did not call us to passivity. He called us to fight...and fight to the death…our own personal death—*my death*. Indeed, it was the method and battle plan that had changed, not God.

As the reconciliation of Old and New Testaments were beginning to make more sense, the whole idea of a Christian "just war" grew more and more ridiculous. However, I have to admit that still, when I read the history of these "saints" from A.D. 400 and 500, such as St. Augustine and Cyril, I was very unsettled. I couldn't help but be intimidated by the vastness of their influence, as well as their antiquity.

However, I was still left with a conspicuous gap in my mental time line. I thought, "Writings from the 400s are agreeably very old, but still, that's more than 375 years after the church began." If Augustine wrote his Just War Theory sometime about A.D. 410, then what did the church do before that? Was this the way the church had always believed?

Chapter Five
The Early Church

Persecution in the Early Church

As the Persian Gulf War drew closer, headlines commonly began to display reports from Kuwait and Iraq suggesting the imminent need for military force. I was rather vocal about my growing convictions, so some of my leaders were beginning to challenge me and ask questions. I welcomed their questions because each time, I secretly wished they would talk me out of all of this.

One afternoon in particular, I remember an intense inward struggle I had while on duty in the armory. Our unit had received a few 203-grenade launchers that we were supposed to attach to some of the M-16 machine guns. Being just back from armory school, it was my job to install them. I vividly remember holding the grenade launcher in my hand, twisting the wire around the M-16 barrel, and asking myself, "What would Jesus do?" The answer seemed clear—of course Jesus would have nothing to do with grenade launchers! But still, I wrestled to justify the whole thing as I put the final touches on the job.

It wasn't long until the whole unit was called into the meeting hall with a tone of urgency one evening. We were given what the commander called our "deadly force briefing." In this meeting, the acting first sergeant was obviously excited. He spoke forcibly as he paced back and forth. This guy was one of those people who dreamed of times like this. His nick-name was "Big Daddy." He was mostly bald and sported a surprisingly tolerated pot belly. It made you wonder how he ever passed the quarterly weigh-ins. Accustomed to using profane words and harsh expressions, he was now explaining the seriousness of the hour and how we were expected to respond to this threat. Then toward the climax of the talk, he looked right at me and said, "If someone tries to get in here you *will* be required to use deadly force to stop him."

Suddenly my funny ideas had become something more than just theological wrangling. I thought to myself, "Well, they can't actually *make* me kill someone. I can just keep this all to myself and walk around looking official." But the more I thought about it, the more convicted I became. My banner of "no compromise" was being tested. And besides the spiritual side of it all, I started to be concerned that if I wasn't being honest with how I was planning to respond to the enemy then I could end up hurting someone else in the unit. My mind was spinning, and my heart was racing.

Cloud of Witnesses

At this time, I think I would have felt completely alone if it had not been for the writings of the early church. I had recently run across a few books that had introduced me to the faith and practice of the early Christians during the first 300 years of the church. The military community in which we were living had many English and American stores off base. One of these was a Christian bookstore with a very unusual assortment of books. I simply couldn't believe what I was finding in this store. It was owned by a regular evangelical minister, but the things that he had in his store were revolutionary. I later found out that he had recently purchased a large portion of his inventory from a local radical bookstore that had gone out of business. This was unfortunate for the man who went out of business, but for me and my wife, it was life changing. One book that I found there was *How Christians Made Peace with War: Early Christian Understandings of War* by John Driver. This book lured me in. I thought this book would help me "make peace" with the war issue, but instead, it introduced me to the writings of the early church.

Other books I found there were volumes by David Bercot, such as *Will the Real Heretics Please Stand Up* and some other primary sources of early Christian writings that David Bercot had published. These books threw open the door showing me that a live, spiritual, powerful church had existed after the death of the apostles.

I had no idea what I was about to find. As I dug into the writings of the early Christians, I soon discovered that the closer I got to the apostles, the simpler, purer, and more biblically literal their teachings became. But more than just doctrine, I found in their writings a faith that caused men to preach from crosses, challenge kings in front of devouring beasts, and caused whole families to lay down their lives for Christ. It seemed that this doctrine of peace and nonresistance flowed naturally from their general understanding of the faith.

The New Kingdom

One of the primary points the early church stressed was that Christ the Messiah had come, and that at His coming He set up His Kingdom in which He alone reigns as King. When the early Christians prayed, "Thy kingdom come, Thy will be done," they meant it! As citizens in that Kingdom, their structure, practices, laws, and even their weapons had been prescribed by their King. I have to admit, as I read the writings of the early Christians, I got excited. These early Christians had such a sense of expectancy. It seemed that they were inspired by watching the fulfillment of the Scriptures right before their eyes.

One of the most significant prophesies, repeated time and time again by the early church was the Kingdom prophecy found in Isaiah:

> "Many people shall come and say, 'Come, and let us go up to the mountain of the LORD, To the house of the God of Jacob; He will teach us His ways, And we shall walk in His paths.' For out of Zion shall go forth the law, And the word of the LORD from Jerusalem. He shall judge between the nations, And rebuke many people; They shall beat their swords into plowshares, And their spears into pruning hooks; Nation shall not lift up sword against nation, Neither shall they learn war anymore."[1]

In fulfillment of this Scripture, they felt that their King had come and done this very thing.

Justin Martyr

Justin Martyr was a philosopher who, after being born again, gave himself to the preaching of Christ until it eventually cost him his life. Writing around A.D. 150, he wrote a debate with a Jewish man in which he appealed to him from the prophesy of Isaiah saying, "We used to be filled with war, mutual slaughter, and every kind of wickedness. However, now all of us have, throughout the whole earth, changed our warlike weapons. We have changed our swords into plowshares, and our spears into farming implements."[2] Later, he wrote a letter to the Emperor, trying to explain Christianity to him. He said, "We who formerly murdered one another now refrain from making war even upon our enemies."[3]

Bishop Irenaeus of Lyons

In another part of the world, an early Christian bishop named Irenaeus, writing a book against polytheists and heretics, explained the way of the Christians:

> "The new covenant that brings back peace and the law that gives life, have gone forth over the whole earth, as the prophets said: "For out of Zion will go forth the law, and the word of the Lord from Jerusalem; and he will rebuke many people; and they will break down their swords into plowshares, and their spears into pruning-hooks, and they will no longer learn to fight."
> ...These people [i.e., Christians] formed their swords and war lances into plowshares...that is, into instruments used for peaceful purposes. So now, they are unaccustomed to fighting. When they are struck, they offer also the other cheek."[4]

I found that, without question, the teaching of nonresistance was an integral part of the faith of the early church, not just from one teacher, or from only one area. Rather, I found that this teaching was preached unanimously from all parts of the ancient world. When I considered that this unity was accomplished without the aid of mass transportation, telephones, or even modern parcel service, it really made me stop and think. Perhaps a literal understanding of Jesus' words was not as crazy as I had once thought.

Clement of Alexandria

Across the Mediterranean, separated by oceans and mountains, was another teacher named Clement of Alexandria, who wrote in about the year A.D. 190. Once again, even there in North Africa, the Gospel he had received was the same. Writing a series of teachings on the Christian faith, Clement explained the faith he had received. In some of those teachings he explained:

- "He bids us to 'love our enemies, bless them who curse us, and pray for those who despitefully use us'. And He says: 'If anyone strikes you on the one cheek, turn to him the other also; and if anyone takes away your coat, do not hinder him from taking your cloak also.'"[5]

- "An enemy must be aided, so that he may not continue as an enemy. For by help, good feeling is compacted and enmity dissolved...We do not train our women like Amazons to manliness in war, for we wish even the men to be peaceable."[6]

- "Christians are not allowed to use violence to correct the delinquencies of sins."[7]

The Early Church Treatment of the Old Testament

What I saw coming out of the early church was the understanding that, without hesitation, they simply believed that Jesus changed the way His Kingdom was to operate and do battle. They emphatically believed that wars and fighting would still continue; it was just that the methods and weapons had changed.

Tertullian

In testifying to how the early Christians viewed this change from the Old Testament practice, Tertullian, a very outspoken early Christian from North Africa, wrote in about A.D. 195:

- "The practice of the old law was to avenge itself by the vengeance of the sword. It was to pluck out 'eye for eye', and to inflict retaliatory revenge for injury. However, the practice of the new law points to mercy."[8]

- "Men of old were used to requiring an 'eye for eye, and tooth for tooth' and to repay evil for evil, with usury!...But after Christ has supervened and has united the grace of faith with patience, now it is no longer lawful to attack others even with words, nor to merely say 'fool', without danger of the judgment...Christ says, 'Love your enemies and bless your cursers, and pray for your persecutors.'"[9]

- "Christ plainly teaches a new kind of long-suffering, when He actually prohibits the reprisals that the Creator permitted in requiring 'an eye for an eye, and a tooth for a tooth.'"[10]

- "Hippias [a pagan] is put to death for laying plots against the state. No Christian ever attempted such a thing on behalf of his brethren, even when persecution was scattering them abroad with every atrocity."[11]

- "For what difference is there between provoker and provoked? The only difference is that the former was the first to do evil, but the latter did evil afterwards. Each one stands condemned in the eyes of the Lord for hurting a man. For God both prohibits and condemns every wickedness. In evil doing, there is no account taken of the order...The commandment is absolute: evil is not to be repaid with evil."[12]

Going beyond personal nonresistance, the early church very clearly taught against killing of any kind, even if it had the guise of a "just" cause. Again, Tertullian challenges:

- "I think we must first inquire whether warfare is proper at all for Christians. What point is there in discussing the merely incidental, when that on which it rests is to be condemned? Do we believe it is lawful for a human oath to be added to one that is divine?...Is it lawful to make an occupation of the sword, when the Lord proclaims that he who uses the sword will perish by the sword? Will the son of peace take part in the battle when it does not become him even to sue at law? Will he who is not the avenger even of his own wrongs apply the chain, the prison, the torture, and the punishment?"[13]

Apostolic Tradition of Hippolytus

During the same time as Tertullian, but in a completely different location, Hippolytus wrote an ancient church document stating guidelines for the church concerning grounds for receiving or rejecting converts into baptism and communion. The church guidelines state, "If an applicant or a believer seeks to become a soldier, he must be rejected, for he has despised God."[14]

You're Not Helping Us

One of the challenges I received from my fellow soldiers was that I was unworthily partaking of the peace that the U.S. Army was giving to me. They asked, "What if everyone in the Army felt this way—what would happen?" They argued that it was not fair for me to enjoy this peace without doing "my part" to maintain it.

This hurt. I had always embraced the idea of doing my part—of being a "team player." I appreciated the sacrifice made by American veterans and what they did for me, but I loved Jesus even more. It wasn't that I despised or disrespected the soldiers. It was that I had undergone a change of allegiance. My allegiance was to Jesus, but I wasn't insensitive to their sacrifices.

Interestingly, I found that the early church was accused of the same thing. Writing about A.D. 248, Origen, another philosopher turned Christian, was giving a defense against this very criticism.

Origen

With faith-filled confidence, Origin challenged his opponents that the Christians were doing a lot more than they thought. The critics of the Christians said that the Christians should feel obligated to labor with them in maintaining justice, and if the need should arise, to fight with them. Origen had a great reply:

> "To this, our answer is that we *do* give help to kings when needed. But this is, so to speak, a divine help, 'putting on the whole armor of God'. And we do this in obedience to the commandment of the apostle: 'I exhort, therefore, that first of all, supplications, prayers, intercessions, and thanksgiving be made for all men; for kings, and for all who are in authority'.
>
> So the more anyone excels in godliness, the more effective the help is that he renders to kings. This is a greater help than what is given by soldiers who go forth to fight and kill as many of the enemy as they can.
>
> Our prayers defeat all demons who stir up war. Those demons also lead persons to violate their oaths and to disturb the peace. Accordingly, in this way, we are much more helpful to the kings than those who go into the field to fight for them.
>
> And we do take our part in public affairs when we join self-denying exercises to our righteous prayers and meditations, which teach us to despise pleasures and not to be led away by them. So none fight better for

the king than we do. Indeed, we do not fight *under* him even if he demands it. Yet, we fight on his behalf, forming a special army—an army of godliness—by offering our prayers to God."[15]

The early church did not need a sword to defend or prosper their cause. The more they were hunted, crucified, fed to lions, or tortured, the more this faith just grew and grew. Speaking about the persecution of Christians, Tertullian told the Romans that instead of diminishing the church, it actually was attracting people to it. Speaking of the result of the empire's merciless persecution of the Christians, he said, "It is bait that wins men for our school. The oftener we are mown down by you, the more in number we grow: the blood of Christians is seed [of the church]."[16]

With sheer bravery, Origen once challenged the Emperor, speaking of the church's growth amid great persecution saying: "And this is in spite of the numerous obstacles that oppose the spread of Christ's teaching in the world. However, since it was the purpose of God that the nations should receive the benefits of Christ's teaching, all the devices of men against Christians have been brought to nothing. For the more that kings, rulers, and peoples have persecuted them everywhere, the more Christians have increased in number and grown in strength."[17]

I was greatly encouraged to discover that the Christians who were the closest to the apostles all agreed unanimously with the literal understanding of Jesus' words, "love your enemies." No "just wars"—just plain and simple, "love your enemies." It was so refreshing!

I thought, "At last I've found some friends and fellowship!" However, it was just too bad for me that they had all died more than 1,700 years ago. There seemed to be such a chasm separating their world from mine. I wondered what had happened. How had the church changed from holding to a universal position of nonresistance, to becoming a military and persecuting force by the time of Augustine? How did such a huge change happen? How was this chasm ever crossed on such a large scale?

Chapter Six
The Constantine Bridge

Constantine's vision

When the idea to build the Brooklyn Bridge across the East River from Brooklyn, New York to Long Island was first conceived, it was met with great skepticism and criticism. One of the greatest obstacles mentioned was the perceived impossibility of laying the foundation towers down into the bedrock under the East River. For millennia, silt and clay had been deposited there, making it nearly impossible to sink a foundation to the rock. Defying the odds, the engineers completed the task by creating a special diving bell equipped with a scooping device that permitted the divers to dig up the silt and clay deep from the river bottom. This allowed them slowly and painfully to reach the bedrock beneath.

Unfortunately, diving to these depths unveiled many mysterious and previously unknown complications for divers. Many of them suffered severe compression sickness, resulting in cramping, paralysis, and even death. Even Washington A. Roebling, the chief architect, died of complications he contracted from the unforgiving power and pressure of the deep.

For me, bridging the chasm between the early church and the modern age seemed just as perilous. The bedrock of doctrines that I found beneath centuries of denominational silt and clay completely altered my life. But as I searched for an explanation of how the church got to where it was in the fifth century, I quickly discovered that a single man, Constantine, had made a tremendous impact on what I was calling the church.

I discovered that regardless of whether historians see Constantine as a benefactor or a spoiler, all of them agree that the bridge spanning the chasm between the persecuted church of the first century and the powerful church of the fifth century rests its foundation towers on the influence of the Emperor Constantine. Without a doubt, Constantine ushered in changes that drastically altered the theology, practice, and political standing of the church. These alterations have endured to the practice of the modern church today.

Background

Near the end of the third century, the church was experiencing a bit of relief from persecution. Christianity was gaining ground, experiencing widespread conversions, reaching even to the Emperor's own family. For a moment, it seemed "safe" to be a Christian. Diocletian had become Emperor, and gifted with a mind for strategy and logistics, he reorganized the Roman Empire into four sections, each run by a separate governing emperor, with himself in the head position. For a while, his plans brought in a greater Roman peace and prosperity.

For the Christians, however, the peace was very brief, and the times of testing soon returned. In A.D. 295, Galerius, one of Diocletian's four new governing emperors, saw to it that a group of Christians be executed for refusing to join the army. Another group of new converts soon followed them, condemned to death for trying to leave the army.

Galerius came against the church in his geographical area. Eventually, he was influential in convincing Diocletian that the Christians could not be trusted to be loyal in any part of the Empire and should therefore be looked on as a threat. By A.D. 303, this influence led to an Empire-wide edict pronounced against the spread and practice of Christianity. With these new laws in place, compounded by a few natural catastrophes, which were conveniently blamed on the Christians, the flames of persecution reached an all-time high. Christians were tortured in an attempt to force them to renounce the faith, surrender holy writings, and worship false gods.

Diocletian Persecution

All across the Empire, the scenes multiplied of courageous, unmovable Christians who refused to cast a pinch of incense into a flickering flame as homage to an idol. For their punishment, they were sentenced to execution by flame and wild beasts. Instead of bowing to false gods, their bodies became fuel for a living sacrifice offered up to the true God of Heaven.

Many heroes and martyrs for Christ emerged during this persecution. Unfortunately, however, not everyone persisted to the end. After a period of toleration and ease in the Empire, the church had grown somewhat lax. When the purifying fires of persecution hit, many, even a large number from the ministry, compromised by turning over sacred copies of the Scriptures. Some even sacrificed to idols. Through it all, the church came into the fourth century limping, dragging theological and political baggage with them.

Predictably, Diocletian's quadrilateral plan to strengthen the Empire did just the opposite—it caused rivalries that led to civil wars. In A.D. 304, Diocletian became sick and by A.D. 305, Galerius took over his section of the Empire, gaining for himself the leading "Augustus" position. During this time, civil wars battered the kingdom back and forth in political chaos for many years. All along, the persecution of Christians raged on.

Soon after Galerius made it to the leading throne, he came down with a painful gastric disease that covered him with ulcers and an "innumerable swarm of devouring insects."[1] Many of the Christians saw this as the judgment of God.

Constantine to the Rescue

Onto this tempestuous scene of momentary prosperity, political chaos, and severe religious persecution entered the opportunistic young ruler, Constantine. Seizing on the chaotic nature of the Empire, Constantine began to design a plan that would allow him to have the Empire as his sole possession.

About A.D. 312, Constantine put his desires into action. In an attack on the unsuspecting armies of Rome, Constantine led 98,000 soldiers from Gaul (present-day France, Belgium, and western Switzerland) across the Swiss Alps and marched on the capital city. On the way to this battle, Constantine had an experience that would change the world forever.

Hoc Vince!

According to the ancient historian, Eusebius, on the day before the battle to take Rome, Constantine reported that he and his men looked up into the sky and saw a vision of a shining cross resting above the sun. Over the cross was the inscription, "By this conquer." Another ancient historian explained that the cross Constantine saw comprised the first two Greek letters of the name of

Christ, X (Chi) and P (Ro).

The next day it is reported that Constantine awoke in a terror when an "angel" exclaimed to him, "Hoc Vince!" which translated means, "By this sign conquer!" Astonishingly, Eusebius claimed that this "angel" was Christ, Himself!

It is reported that Constantine quickly added this X P symbol to the shields of the soldiers. After all these supposedly supernatural events, Constantine met the Roman army led by Emperor Maxentius at the Milvian Bridge, where Constantine's army defeated the local armies of Rome. During the battle, Maxentius fell into the river and drowned. Eusebius records that after Constantine took the city, he ordered that a statue of himself be erected. The statue displayed the XP symbol in his right hand, with the inscription beneath, "By this saving sign, the true token of bravery, I have delivered your city from the yoke of the tyrant."[2]

The First Seeker-Friendly Church

Once the Emperor became supportive of Christianity, people started coming into the church in droves. Christianity was becoming more and more publicly acceptable everywhere. Constantine began rebuilding churches, giving state salaries and tax exemptions to ministers, freeing Christian slaves, and even giving money and new clothes to those who would convert to Christianity. Mass baptisms were conducted all over the Empire, and in the matter of just a few years, literally hundreds of thousands of people came into the church.[3]

Instead of seeing these secular favors as dangerous enticements, most Christians of the day gladly received them without question. Eusebius wrote, "Surely it must seem to all who duly regard these facts that a new and fresh era of existence had begun to appear, and a light heretofore unknown suddenly to dawn from the midst of darkness on the human race: and all must confess that these things were entirely the work of God, who raised up this pious emperor to withstand the multitude of the ungodly."[4]

The more the church accepted these gifts, the faster the gifts came. Some ministers were even invited to dine with Constantine in the Emperor's own palace. Referring to one of these imperial feasts, Eusebius again boasted:

> "On this occasion, public festivals were celebrated by the people of the provinces everywhere, but the emperor himself invited and feasted with those ministers of God whom he had reconciled, and thus offered as it were through them a suitable sacrifice to God. Not one of the bishops was lacking at the imperial banquet, the circumstances of which were splendid beyond description.
>
> Detachments of the bodyguard and other troops surrounded the entrance of the palace with drawn swords, and through the midst of these the men of God proceeded without fear into the innermost of the imperial apartments, in which some were the emperor's own companions at table, while others reclined on couches arranged on either side. One might have thought that a picture of Christ's kingdom was thus shadowed forth, and a dream rather than reality."[5]

But while the bishops and church leaders were feasting in the imperial court, Constantine was busy restructuring the church and the world.

Pontifex Maximus

Constantine was always very interested in religion. The pagan religion of his ancestors was very important to him, especially Apollo the sun god. In A.D. 308, he donated large gifts to the temple of the sun god and obtained the position as the official high priest of the pagan sun god, proudly holding the title "Pontifex Maximus". This position made him the supreme head of the doctrine and practice of the pagan religion throughout the Roman Empire. This was convenient for Constantine; it allowed him to govern even the spiritual and emotional infrastructure of his subjects. Having observed the benefit of its influence on the pagans, Constantine naturally stepped in to govern the affairs of the church as well.

Although Christianity was growing rapidly, paganism still continued strong, especially in the higher classes. Constantine carefully governed both camps by walking a precarious line between paganism and Christianity. As late as A.D. 320, there were Roman coins minted with pagan gods on one side, and the name of Christ on the other. He kept his title as head of the pagan religion until his dying day. Even after his death, the Senate, led by his children, declared him as a new pagan god.[6]

Political Paranoia

In spite of the church's enthusiastic blessing and endorsement in the ever-corrupt political arena, Constantine continued his cut-throat opportunist pursuit. Constantine began to see his brother-in-law, Licinius, as an obvious threat. In an easy defeat, Constantine's army overcame his unsuspecting brother-in-law without much of a fight. Momentarily considerate of family loyalties, Constantine then made a solemn vow to his sister Constance, that he would spare the life of Licinius, her husband, after the invasion. However, in A.D. 325, the very year of the Nicene Council, he broke this vow and had him executed.

After this execution, Constantine's paranoia continued and due to more political suspicions, he eventually had his eleven-year-old nephew executed as well. But most tragically, in A.D. 326, driven nearly crazy by endless jealous surmising, Constantine even had his firstborn son, Crispus, put to death.[7] In his twisted way of thinking, this would prevent any thought of sedition, conspiracy, or possible future overthrow. Yet all along, right through the paganism, scandals, and political atrocities, the church walked hand-in-hand with Constantine, receiving his gifts, favors, and influence.

But what I found even more astounding than the extent of Constantine's physical and monetary influence was the audacious place of leadership and authority that the church so readily handed to him. Constantine was allowed to govern even some of the most sensitive aspects of church polity and doctrine.

Bishop Constantine

Once persecution decreased and comforts increased, the church quickly digressed into substantial parties and divisions, disgracing herself through heated religious debates. When Constantine noticed these divisions, he made it his business to call for a worldwide council of churches to decide various issues. The first of these so-called ecumenical or worldwide councils was held in A.D. 325, in Nicaea, situated in present-day Turkey. The council was held to settle disputes concerning the nature of Christ. However, much more than Christology was discussed there.

Following the pattern of his Roman predecessor, Diocletian, who had geographically divided up the Roman Empire, Constantine divided the entire Christian church into four major geographic areas. He appointed an overseeing bishop called a "Patriarch" or a "Metropolitan" to each of these four areas. Local elders and bishops were now to submit their judgments and decisions to these four metropolitan areas.

In addition to these ecclesiastical changes, specific definitions and doctrinal formulas were drawn up with dogmatic resolves. Those who could not totally go along with the new structure were denied their ecclesiastical positions and privileges.

National unity was crucial to Constantine; groups of Christians who refused the new policies were put out. After the council, Constantine wrote an edict to several of the nonconformists and separatists, calling them "haters of truth." He banished their ministers from office, demanded excommunications, and forbade the nonconformist churches to meet in public, or even in private houses.[8]

Those who compromised the faith by accepting Constantine, saw the king as having a genuine authority within the church. Speaking of Constantine's ecclesiastical office, Eusebius wrote, "He assumed, as it were, the functions of a general bishop, constituted by God and convened synods of His ministers."[9] How the church could have let a non-baptized king, who still openly practiced pagan rites, have a ruling part in the church is incomprehensible.

The Great Abomination

All of this really threw me. I thought, "If the church of that early age would compromise like that, then what would happen today in the face of similar temptation?" I didn't want to sound unbalanced or extreme, but it all sounded an awful lot like the "Great Abomination" prophesied in Revelation 17. In this prophesy, the bride compromises and commits adultery with the kings of the earth. This infidelity thereby produces a defiled hybrid made by joining church and state that eventually grows to persecute the true church. John said in His Revelation:

> "Then one of the seven angels who had the seven bowls came and talked with me, saying to me, "Come, I will show you the judgment of the great harlot who sits on many waters, with whom the kings of the earth committed fornication, and the inhabitants of the earth were made drunk with the wine of her fornication." So he carried me away in the Spirit into the wilder-

ness. And I saw a woman sitting on a scarlet beast which was full of names of blasphemy, having seven heads and ten horns. The woman was arrayed in purple and scarlet, and adorned with gold and precious stones and pearls, having in her hand a golden cup full of abominations and the filthiness of her fornication. And on her forehead a name was written:

MYSTERY, BABYLON THE GREAT, THE MOTHER OF HARLOTS AND OF THE ABOMINATIONS OF THE EARTH.

I saw the woman, drunk with the blood of the saints and with the blood of the martyrs of Jesus. And when I saw her, I marveled with great amazement."[10] (The capital letters are from the original).

Now, I've never been a doomsday-kind-of-guy, nor have I ever bought into a bunch of conspiracy theories. I was never one of those guys who had a problem accepting that Elvis was dead or that Neil Armstrong really walked on the moon. I'm not the kind of guy who just buys into everything radical just because it sounds sensational. But, all that said...this Constantine stuff really scared me.

John said that this "whore of Babylon" was "the mother of harlots." That seems to imply that she has spawned harlot daughters after herself. I asked myself, "Could this mean that a church today which also adulterates the Bride of Christ by joining the church with the kings of the world might very well be considered one of her children—a daughter-harlot of today?"

Now, I didn't want to go too far with this and pass blanket condemnations on the modern church as a whole—but it did make me think. "Saint" Augustine seemed just to accept the hybrid. *Christianity Today* recently quoted Augustine referring to the Bride of Christ saying, "The church is a whore, but she's my mother."[11]

I understand the point they are trying to make, but I'm not at all comfortable with saying that. Jesus said that He is returning for a pure bride, not a harlot. After all, John did conclude his warning about the whore of Babylon with the searing cry, "And I heard another voice from heaven saying, 'Come out of her, my people, lest you share in her sins, and lest you receive of her plagues. For her sins have reached to heaven, and God has remembered her iniquities.'"[12]

Let me say again that I don't feel a need to be the one to pronounce that judgment on any church today, or even in times past. But I do feel that according to John's Revelation, at some point in time, Christians are going to need to discern the times and "come out." As for me, when I considered the changes and compromises that took place under Constantine, I couldn't help but think that for the most part, Christians have waited way too late.

It's Not His Fault

Overall, looking at all these questionable acts of the Emperor Constantine, I couldn't necessarily put the whole blame on him. After all, it was the Bride of Christ—God's people—the church—that had allowed this spiritual adultery to take place. The things with which Constantine was dealing were spiritual things. They could not be governed, reasoned, or manipulated like the affairs of the state. Constantine never even claimed to be converted until he was on his deathbed. It was the church that had willingly traded truth for advantage.

After reading the history of this period, I was very sobered. I realized that I could not simply blame others for any of my own ignorance or deception. The church still will have to answer for compromise and deception today. All the compromises, concessions, and spiritual adulteries that have happened since the time of Constantine are difficult for anyone to ignore. When I considered the church–state hybrid formed from this union way back then, I was astounded at all the damage that had been done.

The Kingdom of God

The need for clarity between the Kingdom of God and the kingdom of this world was becoming painfully conspicuous to me. I saw that the things of the Kingdom of God could be known and understood only through the illumination of the Holy Spirit. Jesus spoke of His Kingdom and salvation to Nicodemus, a leader of the Jewish synagogue. He said: "Verily, verily, I say unto thee, Except a man be born again, he cannot see the kingdom of God" (John 3:3).

What About Me?

I began to realize it was time for me, personally, to decide what I was going to do with these teachings of

Christ, and no longer blame my society, my culture, or my upbringing. Of course, the books I originally gathered from the Army libraries and the chaplain's office did not include all these results of Constantine's pragmatism or Augustine's rationalism. Those first books mainly focused on the idea of Christians defending the innocent to bring about a better good.

The books all admitted—"War is evil." Everyone agreed with that. But the Just War Theory incorporated the idea that although war may indeed be evil, sometimes a lesser evil must be done to bring about the better good. In the books I read, argument after argument was made based on this type of rationalistic thinking.

But now, as I perused through 1,700 years of hindsight, it became obvious that as the church grew in power, influence, and economic stability, it never again spiritually prospered as it once had in its humble, cross-bearing beginnings.

As I continued to search my heart, I began to go beyond the bewilderment of finding out *what* happened in history, to asking *why* it happened, and then, *why* it continues to happen now. In doing this, God revealed even deeper areas in my life that needed to be turned over to Him.

Chapter Seven
Why?

During the time of the Reformation (1500–1550), God's light was being poured out in many miraculous and unexpected ways. Some people responded with theological reform. Some radically changed their lifestyle, and still others poured themselves into missions. One of those men was a missionary by the name of Francis Xavier. In 1549, by the request of a fugitive Samurai warrior named Anjiro, Xavier sailed to Japan to plant a church. He was very successful, and it was said of these converts that they were very zealous.

Interestingly, when Francis Xavier asked Anjiro if he thought Japan would receive Christianity, he replied, "They would not do so immediately, but would first ask you many questions and see what you knew. Above all, they would want to see whether your life corresponded with your teaching."

Gary G. Kohls who wrote about this period tells us that Christianity took root there. But in the 1600s, it quickly became the target of brutal Japanese Imperial persecutions. Within 50 years after the planting of Xavier's mission church, it was a capital crime to be a Christian in Japan. The Japanese Christians who refused to recant their beliefs suffered ostracism, torture, and even crucifixions similar to the Roman persecutions in the first three centuries of Christianity. After the reign of terror was over, it appeared to all observers that Christianity had been completely stamped out.

However, 250 years later, Japan was being opened up for trade purposes, and it was discovered that thousands of baptized Christians still existed in Nagasaki, Japan. It was now the 1850s, and these Christians were living their faith in a catacomb existence, in caves and homes, completely unknown to the government. When they were identified, the government started another series of persecutions. However, this time, because of international pressures, the persecutions were soon stopped, and Nagasaki Christianity came up from the underground.

In a relatively short time, by 1917, the Japanese Christians had organized and built a massive Cathedral, calling it St Mary's. By the 1940s, thousands of people professed to be Christians in Japan. It appeared to most that Christianity was beginning to be practiced openly, without fear of hostility and persecution.

However, early in the morning of August 9, 1945, a few young American Christians from another part of the world met with two chaplains—one Lutheran and the other Catholic—for a little prayer meeting before they started their day's work. After the prayer, these two American Christians climbed into their B-29 Super Fortress long-distance bomber and began heading from Tinian Island to Nagasaki with orders to drop the second atomic bomb.

Tragically, history records that St. Mary's Cathedral was one of the very landmarks these American Christians had been told to look for as they flew into the target zone. Shortly after the pilot identified the cathedral, he ordered the atom bomb to be dropped.

At 11:02 a.m., as told in Kohl's words, "Nagasaki Christianity was boiled, evaporated, and carbonized in a scorching, radioactive fireball. The persecuted, vibrant, faithful, surviving center of Japanese Christianity had become ground zero. And what the Japanese Imperial government could not do in over 200 years of persecu-

tion, American Christians did in nine seconds."[1] The
Christians of Nagasaki were wiped out.

Why?

Almost immediately, the war was over. America was
now seen as the ultimate world superpower. America
could call the shots, set up summits of world leaders,
demand treaties, and control whole nations—but at
what cost? In the minds of most western Christians,
might and power had won. To be strong was to survive.
To be brave, bold, and confident became not only the
mindset of secular America, but of the church as well.
The long-forgotten verses, "blessed are the meek" and,
"blessed are the peacemakers" became even further re-
legated to not much more than a nice decoration for
pretty little gilded placemats and souvenir ash trays.

Admittedly, some of the men who literally "pulled
the trigger" felt that perhaps this time, we had gone too
far. Albert Einstein said, "I made one great mistake in
my life—when I signed the letter to President Roosevelt
recommending that atom bombs be made."

J. Robert Oppenheimer, the actual inventor of the
atom bomb, said, "The atomic bomb made the prospect
of future war unendurable. It has led us up those last
few steps to the mountain pass; and beyond there is a
different country."

Even five-star General Douglas MacArthur, in a
speech given at the surrender of the Japanese after
Hiroshima and Nagasaki, said, "Military alliance,
balances of power, League of Nations all in turn
failed...We have had our last chance. If we do not now
devise some greater and more equitable system,

Armageddon will be at our door. The problem basically is theological and involves a spiritual recrudescence and improvement of human character that will synchronize with our almost matchless advance in science, art, literature and all material and cultural developments of the past two thousand years. It must be of the spirit if we are to save the flesh."

These were some great confessions, and admittedly, it was good that men were recognizing the need for compassion for humanity. Yet, ironically, the words of Christ and His narrow way only drifted further off, as nonresistant ideals were to be espoused only by the secular humanist and the intellectual idealist. As for the church, "might is right" had now solidified to the point of dogma.

Being Honest

The facts of war had really unsettled me further. Just as the Berlin Wall had challenged me to realize that I could not wait for secular leaders to choose my enemies and allies, military acts such as the bombing of Nagasaki and Hiroshima graphically demonstrated to me what happens when the Kingdom of God and the kingdom of this world mix.

As I studied to understand, I found that the historians always cited very good reasons and justification for each case. All of them, from Augustine and the Donatists, to the Crusaders against Islam during the Middle Ages, to the tyranny of Stalin and Hitler, the ones doing the extinguishing always cited good, pragmatic justification for every cause. Yet, more and more my cry was becoming, "Christian beware! The age-old adage bears a grave truth—'The victors write the history books!'"

A Few Definitions

Simply defined *pragmatism* is "whatever works—is what is right." *Utilitarianism* can be defined as "what is right—is whatever is best for the greatest number of people." Both of these concepts imbibe the idea of *expediency,* which is "what is right—is whatever is convenient for the immediate situation."

Built right into the American psyche, these three ideologies—pragmatism, utilitarianism, and expediency—reign as philosophical fundamentals. As a good American boy, these concepts were well ingrained in me. My childhood dreams were filled with ideas of climbing the ladder of success. Growing up, I felt that getting ahead, making the grade, and paying my dues would lead me on the path to achieve the American dream—"life, liberty, and the pursuit of happiness." Now, however, I was discovering that if I actually wanted to experience the fulfillment of God's promises in my life, these pragmatic ideologies were three giants that needed to be slain.

To turn away from this type of thinking was not easy for my wife and me. As we continued coming to the Lord, we soon discovered that everything around us— our culture, our friends, and our profession—had all been dictated more by expediency than anything else. I found my own society's lifeblood flowed to the beats and demands of valueless pragmatism.

As I continued to ask why and how all the war and bloodshed continued to happen century after century, even in the church, the answer became obvious. When biblical truths are lost and the ultimate goal of society becomes personal gratification and the pursuit of happiness, then greed and selfishness are all that is left. With this mindset, conflicts and wars are inevitable. If the pursuit of happiness is the ultimate goal, then naturally, when another person or society threatens to interfere with my happiness, then any measures necessary to preserve this end appear justifiable. Hence, nuclear-equipped armies called "Peacekeepers" or multilayered national task forces labeled "Home Land Security" become reasonable means to achieve these ends, regardless of the moral or financial cost.

As I continued to study, it became painfully obvious that it was professing "Christians" who were behind some of the worst atrocities, wars, and crimes in history. I thought, "This type of moral ambiguity and uncertainty all is understandable coming from a people who believe we are no more than 'organisms' evolved from cosmic space-matter, or from faithless unbelievers whose final hope is only in this life—but coming from the people who claim to follow the only living, personal, and benevolent God, it is an inexcusable tragedy."

The Reason For War

The book of James asks the ultimate war question, "Whence come wars and fightings among you?" I found his answer profound, "Do they not come from your desires for pleasure that war in your members? You lust and do not have. You murder and covet and cannot obtain. You fight and war. Yet you do not have because you do not ask. You ask and do not receive, because you ask amiss, that you may spend it on your pleasures."[2]

When Jesus came to earth, He spoke and taught often of the "Kingdom of God." Jesus revealed to the world a radical, diametrically different underlying and guiding principle that was much more than personal gratification and the pursuit of happiness. In His Kingdom, the all-encompassing goal is not *our* happiness and earthly accomplishments, but rather an all-out pursuit to love God and to glorify Him with every aspect of our lives.

In His Kingdom, our entire lives, including our ambitions, happiness, decisions, and desires are consumed to this end—to glorify God. When the angels proclaimed the birth of Jesus, they sang, "Glory to God in the Highest!" The Apostle Paul said, "For of him, and through him, and to him, are all things: to whom be glory forever. Amen."[3]

As I read through many of the Army books attempting to justify the Christian's place in war and self-defense, I began to notice a common thread. In these military, theological, and historical books, war was often likened to the surgeon's knife or the farmer's hoe. The need to defend the innocent, the helpless, and the "just" outweighed all the evil acts of war. Even questionable acts, such as the nuclear bombing of civilian women and children in Hiroshima and Nagasaki during World War II, were defended as "just" and "right." Yet, in spite of all the rationale, as much as I tried, I just could not let go of the simple, albeit impractical words of Jesus—"Love your enemies, do good to them that hate you."

But now, as Tania and I endeavored to live out these "new" ideals for the first time, our commitment to them was challenged right from the start. When my wife and I made up our minds to leave the Army, we were met with the overwhelming reality that we had suddenly lost all of our support. Losing our careers was just the beginning. Thinking it through, we realized we would be giving up all that we had labored so hard to achieve. We often trembled as we watched our lives seemingly fall apart before our very eyes.

It wasn't easy to say good-bye to our health insurance, retirement, college money, rent payment, bank account, church, friends—all of life as we had known it. And as time went on, there were moments when we really were tempted to despair. But as the anxiety from this realization began to mount and at times loom over us, we were forced to take a hold of God's promises. We had no choice but either to turn completely back or to take the Lord at His Word. It was a comfort to know that we certainly were not the first Christians to find ourselves in such a place. It was inspiring to remember that we simply were following in the footsteps of many others who had gone before us.

Personal Need

During this time, I believe God was taking us beyond the surface of the mere doctrines of peace and war to the recognition of a deeper need in our life—the need for security and self-sufficiency. As I continued reading the Scriptures and praying, the source of my confusion became clear to me. I slowly began to realize that I had allowed "pragmatic thinking" to creep in and destroy many areas of my life by minimizing the promises of God and teachings of the Bible. "Seek first the kingdom of God and His righteousness, and all these things shall be added to you"[4] had always been a beautiful verse to me—one that I knew by heart. But it wasn't a reality in my life.

My flesh, or human instinct, argued that a lesser evil could be done to bring about a better good. But as I studied the Word of God, I found that God was vehemently opposed to such teaching. My flesh cried out, "The end justifies the means!" But I found that God was just as concerned with *how* I did things as He was with why I was doing them. Proverbs 16:25 says, "There is a way that seems right to a man, But its end is the way of death." Paul, writing to the Christians in Rome stated, "And why not say, 'Let us do evil that good may come'?—as we are slanderously reported and as some affirm that we say. Their condemnation is just."[5] I saw that throughout Bible history God's heart has desired to have a people who put their trust completely in Him.

Example From Abraham

Thousands of years ago, God called Abraham at a very old age to leave his home, friends, and way of life to follow Him through unknown lands, based on promises from God—promises that He would give him a son and take him to a land "flowing with milk and honey." God was so pleased with Abraham's faith that He gave Abraham the name "Friend of God."

The Apostle Paul, speaking of Abraham's powerful trust in God's promises, said of him, "He staggered not at the promise of God through unbelief; but was strong in faith, giving glory to God; And being fully persuaded that, what he had promised, he was able also to perform. And therefore it was imputed to him for righteousness" (Romans 4:20–22).

One central point of God's call to Abraham was that He was going to provide Abraham with an heir. But when the fulfillment of the promise tarried, Abraham was tempted to lose heart. Coming back from the battle after rescuing his brother Lot, Abraham met with Melchizedek. Shortly after this meeting, God came to Abraham and renewed his vision, telling him, "Do not be afraid, Abram. I am your shield, your exceedingly great reward."[6]

Encouraged by his renewed communication, Abraham cried out to God with the burden of his heart. Now, at the age of 86 years, he had begun to grow discouraged because the promise of an heir was not fulfilled. So he reasoned that God must have meant not a real son, but a servant born in his house, thus fulfilling the promise in principle only. Abraham did not feel he directly denied the promise by compromising in this way, but in effect, he diminished its efficacy and power by leaning on his own human reasoning.

Like Abraham, I am constantly tempted to redefine God's promises. When I read in Scripture, "Seek ye first the kingdom of God, and his righteousness; and all these things shall be added unto you,"[7] it is easy for me to turn it into some kind of legal or pretended fulfillment instead of an actual reality in my life. But God assured Abraham, "This one shall not be your heir, but one who will come from your own body shall be your heir."[8] God's promise was fulfilled in reality, not by a mere legality.

The revelation and reassurance Abraham received from this angel gave him clarity and renewed his faith. But as the years continued to pass, the possibility of a real fulfillment began to grow more and more unrealistic. Frustration surfaced, and Sarah offered her bond slave, Hagar, to Abraham as a practical, human means to fulfill the promise. This time, the mistake did not stop with just mental temptations to doubt God's promise.

The fruit of Abraham's compromise was Ishmael. After Hagar conceived, she immediately felt superior to Sarah and started to despise her. Later, when Isaac was born by the miraculous fulfillment of God's promise, the contention and jealousy proliferated. Ishmael grew in jealousy and persisted in persecuting Isaac incessantly. There was no way for them to live together peaceably, so Ishmael and Hagar eventually were driven out.

In time, Ishmael's descendents moved to the east and south of the promised land and came to be known collectively as the Arabs. Still today, 4,000 years later, the conflict between the descendants of Sarah and the descendants of Hagar rages on, making international news as they continue to fight. Oh, what damage results when human means are used to accomplish God's promises!

Rise and Walk

There is an old story from the 13th century about a surprise meeting between the famed theologian, Thomas Aquinas, and Pope Innocent II. As the story goes, one day Aquinas came upon Pope Innocent II as he was taking inventory of the church treasury. The pope was right in the middle of counting a few large stacks of silver and gold coins when Aquinas came walking in. Looking up to Aquinas, the pope said:

"You see Thomas—the church no longer needs to say 'silver and gold have I none.'"

"This is true," Thomas Aquinas quickly replied, "and neither can she say, 'arise and walk!'"

History has demonstrated time and time again that when the church stops trusting in God and begins to rely on its own strength and resources, failure and compromise always follow. God was showing me that the reasons for war, fighting, lust, and corruption are the same now as they always have been—they result from trusting man more than God, by putting man first. I concluded that all the passions, pleasures, and pride of man will never form a peaceful society, regardless how liberated and democratic it may claim to be.

James sternly finishes his ultimate war question, "Whence come wars and fightings among you?" with this strong admonition, "Whoever therefore wants to be a friend of the world makes himself an enemy of God. Or do you think that the Scripture says in vain, 'The Spirit who dwells in us yearns jealously'? But He gives more grace. Therefore He says: 'God resists the proud, But gives grace to the humble.'"[9] I wanted to be like Abraham—to trust fully and even foolishly in God's promises to the point that I too might be called a friend of God.

Chapter Eight
Excuses

Tania and I in front of the band hall in Germany

As I contemplated the direction that these new ideas were taking, I felt that my own personal needs, my own fears, and my own general welfare had been enough to worry about. However, all of my big ideas became tougher when I considered how these things would affect my wife and family. When it was all said and done, taking the words of Christ at face value was a real challenge for me—it still is. It's a lot easier for me to decide about right or wrong—good or bad—by the way I feel about something, or by how it affects my immediate little world. If certain teachings of Jesus don't fit into my world, I find it all too easy simply to ignore them, or to attempt to explain them away theologically.

But that's exactly what makes the Bible confusing. I had to be honest. Many of the things I was trying to hold onto, or explain away, took quite a lot of exegetical gymnastics. I finally came to see that if Jesus could say something as straightforward as "love your enemies," and I could turn it into support for atomic warfare, then who could blame people for saying that the Bible was confusing!

Talking With Others

I found that when I started discussing controversial subjects such as war and nonresistance with others, most people wanted to get away from the Scriptures as quickly as possible. It's hard to argue with words such as, "If your enemy is hungry, feed him." Usually, in such a debate, the attention went to a list of several hypothetical scenarios or consequences. Arguments such as, "Do you realize what would happen if everybody did that?" or "What do you think would happen if every Christian left the Army?" Critics were not concerned with what the Scriptures said, but rather, attempted to make a case to show why the scriptures simply can't be saying what they obviously say.

This type of rationalizing is not new. Even in Jesus' day, when Jesus called people to His way of life, the result was similar: "And they all with one consent began to make excuses" (Luke 14:18).

I tried to ignore these arguments but I couldn't. I actually was amazed to find that these hypothetical stories and scenarios actually had a stronger effect on people's theology than anything else. If I wanted to get my point across, then I had to face up to these hypothetical scenarios, whether I liked it or not.

What if Someone is Attacking Your Family?

One of the most common "scenario questions" had to do with protecting my family. This one strikes a deep chord in all of us. We all love our families, and most would do just about anything to protect them. The critics argue that all of this "turning-the-other-cheek stuff" is okay if it involves only me, but if a loved one is being hurt, then we should be willing to commit a lesser evil to protect the innocent. They typically cite the common misunderstanding: "I cannot just sit there and do nothing!"

The Question

The standard argument, although it may differ somewhat in the details, usually goes something like this:

"What would you do if someone came into your house and was trying to attack your wife or children? Would you shoot the attacker to protect your family, or would you just sit there and do nothing and watch them die?"

In trying to answer, I found that these questions came with a few built-in traps. Besides the obvious play on emotion, one of the main problems with this type of question is the narrow set of choices offered. In real life, Christians have found several possibilities other than the limited ones offered in these hypothetical scenarios—such as putting themselves in harm's way, fleeing the scene, or even prayer.

Another trap is the setting itself. Often the setting is unrealistic or places the Christian in a situation that he probably could have—or should have—avoided in the first place.

One of the books I found in Germany that really helped me with these questions was a book by John H. Yoder entitled *What Would You Do?* In his discussion Yoder hits this line of thinking head-on. Addressing how to answer these types of questions, Yoder writes:

> "How do we answer the question? We must note, first of all, that the questioner wants us to answer simply either yes or no. For most questioners, the only choices which the question offers are defense—which must necessarily be lethal—and nondefense, which is sure to permit the worse to happen. But this is a wildly illogical way to pose the problem."[1]

Yoder exposes that the questioner in these hypothetical scenarios usually tries to force a response of kill or not kill. He argues that there certainly are several more possible outcomes than these two. Highlighting the inconsistencies that saturate these types of questions, Yoder offers a somewhat comical dialog written by Joan Baez entitled "Three Cheers for Grandma!"

Three Cheers for Grandma!

"Okay, you're a pacifist. What would you do if someone were, say, attacking your grandmother?"

"Attacking my poor old grandmother?"

"Yeah. You're in a room with your grandmother, and there's this guy about to attack her, and you're standing there. What would you do?"

"I'd yell, 'Three cheers for Grandma'! and leave the room."

"No, seriously. Say he had a gun, and he was about to shoot her. Would you shoot him first?"

"Do I have a gun?"

"Yes."

"No. I'm a pacifist; I don't have a gun."

"Well, say you do."

"All right. Am I a good shot?"

"Yes."

"I'd shoot the gun out of his hand."

"No, then you're not a good shot."

"I'd be afraid to shoot. Might kill grandma."

"Come on. Okay, look. We'll take another example. Say you're driving a truck. You're on a narrow road with a sheer cliff on your side. There's a little girl standing in the middle of the road. You're going too fast to stop. What would you do?"

"I don't know. What would you do?"

"I'm asking you. You're the pacifist."

"Yes, I know. All right. Am I in control of the truck?"

"Yes."

"How about if I honk my horn so she can get out of the way?"

"She's too young to walk. And the horn doesn't work."

"I swerve around to the left of her since she's not going anywhere."

"No , there's been a landslide."

"Oh. Well, then, I would try to drive the truck over the cliff and save the little girl."

Silence.

"Well, say there's someone else in the truck with you. Then what?"

"What's my decision have to do with my being a pacifist?"

"There's two of you in the truck and only one little girl."

"Someone once said, 'If you have the choice between a real evil and a hypothetical evil, always take the hypothetical one'."

"Huh?"

"I said why are you so anxious to kill off all the pacifists?"

"I'm not. I just want to know what you'd do."

"If I were with a friend in a truck driving very fast on a one-lane road approaching a dangerous impasse where a ten-month-old girl is sitting in the middle of the road with a landslide on one side of her and a sheer drop-off on the other?"

"That's right."

"I would probably slam on the brakes, thus sending my friend through the front windshield, skid into the landslide, run over the little girl, sail off the cliff, and plunge to my own death. No doubt grandma's house would be at the bottom of the ravine, and the truck would crash through her roof and blow up in her living room, where she was finally being attacked for the first, and last, time."

"You haven't answered my question. You're just trying to get out of it."

"I'm really trying to say a couple of things. One is that no one knows what he'll do in a moment of crisis. And that hypothetical questions get hypothetical answers. I'm also hinting that you have made it impossible for me to come out of the situation without having killed one or more people. Then you say 'Pacifism is a nice idea, but it won't work.'"[2]

Doesn't Faith Mean Anything?

From a purely secular mindset, the dichotomy "kill or do nothing" might have some merit, but not for the man of faith. Those "other possible responses" are precisely what will distinguish the Christian man from the man who has no hope.

Yoder says it is striking when you read the many biographies of missionaries who weren't even schooled in an explicit theology of nonresistance to see that when they actually were placed in one of these "hypothetical" situations, they almost instinctively assumed it would be wrong to resort to violence to protect their families. What's more amazing, even in the face of such danger, they testify of a clear expectation of God's deliverance. Leaving room for God to work miracles in such situations has propagated the faith for centuries.[3]

In the end, I found that the question of my family's security actually is a matter of faith. If I really believe Jesus meant it when he said I am to love my enemies, then looking for excuses why I can't obey His word is not an option. Instead, I should be looking to Him for the grace I need to live up to something like this.

David Bercot in his book *The Kingdom That Turned the World Upside-Down* touched on the point of Christian faithfulness saying:

> "What if a foreign government ordered me to drop a bomb on a United States city or to assassinate the American president–or else they would harm my wife and children? What should I do? I think most Americans would allow their wives and children to be harmed, or even killed, before betraying their country.
>
> So how is the situation any different when it concerns loyalty to Jesus? Jesus' teachings on nonresistance are quite clear. It's a matter of either denying Him or denying my family. To be sure, that's a very difficult choice, but I already made that choice when I gave my life to Christ.
>
> Does that mean I would do nothing to protect my family? Of course not. I have already done the best thing that I could possibly do to ensure their safety: I have entrusted my home and family to the care and protection of Jesus. And that

isn't some naive trust. There are tens of thousands of other Kingdom Christians who have similarly beat their swords into plowshares and entrusted the safety of their families into the hands of their King. And although Jesus has not promised that no harm can ever come to our families, I can say this: that, except in times of religious persecution, it's very rare for kingdom families to be harmed by ordinary criminals."[4]

Collateral Damage

One of the most unfair things about the "save-your-grandma" line of reasoning is its play on emotions. Obviously, the idea of my family getting killed is simply unthinkable. But is it not profoundly ironic to compare this with modern warfare? I mean, it's not like innocent families are not getting killed during war. As a matter of fact, the military has a name for these helpless victims. They call these dead men, women, and children "collateral damage."

The sad reality is that whether it be premeditated war or loving our enemies, tragedies happen and people die. Emotional plays won't change that. I may not know how I will respond to every overwhelming situation that I will face in my future. But I know how I *want* to respond—I know how I am *supposed* to respond—like Christ. He has promised me that by His grace I can do that. Premeditated disobedience to the teaching of Christ, however, is not an option. And that is exactly what this line of thinking is suggesting.

Closing this section in his book, Bercot cites an example of a miraculous deliverance for a couple that he knows personally:

> "A number of years ago, some Christian friends of mine, Decio and Olivia, were staying at a motel in Atlanta. There had been a number of armed robberies and murders in the city. In these robberies, the assailants had ordered their victims to lie face down on the floor and then shot them in the backs of their heads. So Decio was on his guard.
>
> It was a mild October evening, and Decio and Olivia had momentarily left their motel door open for a friend. Suddenly two teenage thugs appeared in the doorway with guns. They ordered everyone down on the floor. Decio hesitated and then knelt down, praying and trying to think of a way to foil the robbery.
>
> His wife, Olivia, thinking it was a Halloween prank, remained seated on the bed. So one of the young robbers waved his gun at her and ordered her to lie on the floor. Instead, she started singing out loud "Jesus Loves Me," as she got up from the bed and slowly walked over to the two young men. One of them raised his pistol, pointed it at her face, and cocked it. But when she continued singing and walking toward him, he suddenly yelled to his partner, "These are a bunch of Jesus nuts! Let's get outta here!" And with that, the two young men vanished into the dark.
>
> Over the years, I have heard and read many other accounts of how a prayer, a hymn, or a

testimony effectively disarmed a would-be burglar or assailant. There's no point singing "Our God Is an Awesome God," if we don't really believe that He is."[5]

Ouch!

Arguments From Silence

Strangely enough, another one of the most common objections to Christian nonresistance I discovered was the "argument of silence." In what looked to me like a desperate grasping at straws, many books and Christian friends defended Christian warfare based almost entirely on a case of "silence."

The two "silent scenes" quoted most often from the Bible were the conversion of the centurion in Acts 10 and the command of John the Baptist to the Roman soldiers.

The Centurion

In Acts 10, Peter was prompted by the Holy Spirit to bring the Gospel to a devout, searching centurion named Cornelius. The centurion and his entire household were quickly converted. Peter even reports that the Holy Spirit was miraculously poured out on all of them, just as it had been at Pentecost. This was an amazing miracle.

But the account nowhere mentions that Cornelius' family received instructions about nonresistance or "loving your enemies." Never mind the fact that there also is no mention that his family or servants received instruction concerning idols, fornication, gladiator shows, or even emperor worship. The account just tells us that the "whole household" got converted. But, because "love your enemies" was not mentioned, friends and theologians deduce that Christian warfare is okay.

John The Baptist

The other most common objection based on silence centers on John the Baptist. According to Luke 3, John was baptizing people in the wilderness. Many people were coming to him asking, "What shall we do?" The two people mentioned in this scriptural account were the tax collector and the Roman soldiers. Modern theologians, grasping for straws, say that John didn't tell them to stop killing people or even to get out of the Army. Therefore, they insist that it must be okay to kill people as long as you are doing it as a soldier.

Concerning this argument, I came to realize a very significant point — John The Baptist was an Old Testament prophet. As a matter of fact, he was the very *last* of the Old Testament prophets. Luke says "The law and the prophets were until John." But then He says — and this was the point that got me — "Since that time the kingdom of God has been preached, and everyone is pressing into it" (Luke 16:16). It is significant that Jesus said that the preaching of the Kingdom of God came *after* John. Only *after* John did people began to press into the Kingdom.

Now bear in mind that John the Baptist was no ordinary Old Testament prophet. Jesus says that he was the greatest of them all, "Verily I say unto you, Among them that are born of women there hath not risen a greater than John the Baptist." This means that John was better than Moses, better than Elijah, better than Jeremiah, and even better than David! But most significantly, Jesus then tells us that this great prophet, who was the greatest man ever born of women, is not as great as he that is the *least* in the Kingdom of Heaven! I had to stop and consider these profound words: "Notwithstanding he that is least in the kingdom of heaven is greater than he" (Matthew 11:11).

I want to be in *that* Kingdom! I don't want to stand on an "argument of silence"—I want to stand on the words of Christ!

Taking It Seriously

I tried very hard to accept these "silent arguments." However, I found that between me and these "silent arguments" were the deafening cries of dead multitudes killed at the hands of those who professed to be "followers of Christ." Between me and these "silent arguments" stood the hindsight of 1,500 years of gruesome mistakes done in the name of "just" causes. And most disturbing, between me and these "silent arguments" stood the unmistakably plain and deafening words of Jesus Christ—"love your enemies."

In addition, as I continued to analyze these arguments, I realized that to accept this defense for warfare, I would basically have to negate Jesus' clear command "love your enemies" based on arguments of silence.

Jesus' sobering words at the end of His Sermon on the Mount make it painfully clear that His teachings are not mere suggestions or quaint meditations. He plainly declares that He is ushering in His new Kingdom, and that many will give excuses on that day. He gives us a frightening warning:

> "Not everyone who says to Me, 'Lord, Lord,' shall enter the kingdom of heaven, but he who does the will of My Father in heaven. Many will say to Me in that day, 'Lord, Lord, have we not prophesied in Your name, cast out demons in Your name, and done many wonders in Your name?' And then I will declare to them, 'I never knew you; depart from Me, you who practice lawlessness!'
>
> Therefore whoever hears these sayings of Mine, and does them, I will liken him to a wise man who built his house on the rock: and the rain descended, the floods came, and the winds blew and beat on that house; and it did not fall, for it was founded on the rock. But everyone who hears these sayings of Mine, and does not do them, will be like a foolish man who built his house on the sand: and the rain descended, the floods came, and the winds blew and beat on that house; and it fell. And great was its fall" (Matthew 7:20–27).

As for me, I realized I could no longer make excuses. I wanted to follow my King, and Him alone! I wanted to be one of "the least of these" in the Kingdom of Heaven! Now I could truly sing:

> On Christ the solid Rock I stand,
> All other ground is sinking sand;
> All other ground is sinking sand!

Chapter Nine
The Pilgrim Church

Early Anabaptists having church in a boat

What do you do when you wake up in a world you have lived in all your life and suddenly, as hard as you try, you just can't fit in anymore? I talked to friends and co-workers constantly, but I always got the same strange glassy-eyed "you're-taking-it-too-far" look. One of my good Christian friends on the base was concerned about me and came one day saying, "Dean, you're asking questions that should never be asked." I asked him how he dealt with the words of Jesus concerning our enemies, and he replied that he was "comfortable."

"Comfortable?" I was far from comfortable. I had the sensation that I was walking about in a sleeping world trying to arouse anyone who would listen—but no one would wake up. It was lonely. I have to admit that in those days my wife and I often longed just to go back to sleep with the rest of them. Thanks be to the Lord, His grace continued to illuminate our path.

Although we were living in Germany, our church at that time was a very large, English-speaking church involving several U.S. military bases. When the Persian Gulf War was warming up, the sermons were beginning more and more frequently to defend the idea of Christians in warfare. One night the church planned a special meeting to which they invited in a former pacifist to speak to us about the Christian's place in war. He used all the same pragmatic reasoning I had heard before, but this time, in addition to the old rhetoric, he also added his own testimony of how he had come to this knowledge.

As he spoke, others joined in and shared how they had been misunderstood as Christians because people did not think they would make good fighting soldiers.

One pilot even stood and shared, almost weeping, how he believed that he was not allowed to be a fighter pilot because during his training period his commander did not understand his Christian convictions. He enthusiastically charged the congregation that people need to understand that Christians have no problems with jobs such as those performed by dive-bombers and fighter-pilots. Throughout the night, many an "Amen" was heard resonating throughout the church. And often a look came my way as if to see what I was thinking.

Then came the moment of truth...the pastor went up with the speaker and after giving him many accolades and confirmations, proclaimed that he felt this should pretty well close the issue. Backed with renewed confidence, he said that if the congregation had any corrections or questions for him, they should ask them now. This was my chance! All through his talk I had been thinking of scriptures and historical facts and here was my chance to stand and proclaim a different view. A few who knew my feelings looked my way, and I tried with everything I had in me to raise my hand.

"Any more questions?" the pastor asked. I knew this was my last chance. My mind was spinning. There was so much I wanted to challenge, but how could I put it into "a question"? As I sat there trying to organize a question, the time was up, and the pastor began the closing prayer. I felt horrible. The whole experience sealed the reality of what I was feeling—I was alone.

Maybe They're Right?

The next day, I called the church office and set up an appointment with the pastor. My goal was a last ditch effort for him to convince Tania and me that we were wrong.

The meeting didn't go very well. Every time I brought up a question the pastor said, "You're not going to change my mind."

We assured him saying, "It is not our goal to change your mind; we just have some questions."

I asked him, "What do you do with the teachings of Jesus on this subject, you know, words like "love your enemies"?

Without any discussion he just shook his head and repeated, "You're not going to change my mind." And then, the final words…sort of looking down, he said "Perhaps you would be more comfortable worshiping elsewhere."

Sometimes I'm a bit slow to recognize when someone is telling me to beat it…so I asked another question. He simply repeated his resolute advice… "Perhaps you would be more comfortable worshiping elsewhere."

This time, I got it. We thanked him for his time and left. I think it was not until we got home that we realized we no longer had a church. We felt alone. It was painful, confusing, and even scary—but oh, how dear Jesus became to us during this time.

Strangers and Pilgrims

The words of Hebrews exhorted me, teaching me that the only way to keep going through times such as this was to keep my eyes on the nonchanging promises of God, as others had always done before me.

"These all died in faith, not having received the promises, but having seen them afar off, and were persuaded of them, and embraced them, and confessed that they were strangers and pilgrims on the earth."[1]

The testimony of the saints that lived before me became more than just a comfort or a historical curiosity. For a time, they became my church. The unanimous voice of the church on this subject during her first 300 years was a real strength for me, against what seemed to be a nearly universal opposing voice in the modern church. However, as comforting as this was, I still felt there had to be more than just the early church. I had to believe that if this all was true, then honest believers throughout time, led by the Spirit of God, would have read the Scriptures and come to the same conclusions.

As I studied on, I began to get excited. Some of the books I was reading at this time not only told of the faith of the early church, but went on to show how many groups of Christians down through the ages have kept these truths, even in spite of severe persecution. David Bercot's *Will The Real Heretic Please Stand Up*, John Kennedy's *The Torch of The Testimony*, and E. H. Broadbent's *The Pilgrim Church*, were some of the volumes that traced many of the ancient beliefs of the apostles down through the ages.

I found that throughout the centuries, Christians who trusted in the promises of God and dared to live by His ways have gathered together to worship God in truth. Even before Constantine, as the church grew lax and began to compromise with the world, groups of believers gathered together desiring a church that sought for purity.

Waldensians

A remarkable group of radical Christian believers that impressed me was the Waldensians. Many separated groups of radical believers have felt one with them. Some writers have even attempted to trace them all the way back to the apostles. Formally, their origin is generally traced back to a rich merchant turned radical preacher named Valdes, otherwise known as Peter Waldo.

In A.D. 1174, Peter Waldo came across the teaching of Jesus and was particularly impressed with the story of the rich young ruler. After a dramatic conversion, he left his merchant life, gave his money to the poor, and began living a radical life for Jesus. During a famine in A.D. 1176, he started a soup kitchen to feed the poor. After this famine, he began his vocation as an itinerant preacher.

The early Waldensians lived a life of radical self-sacrifice and voluntary poverty. Motivated by Jesus' teaching to evangelize and preach the Gospel, they sent out preachers across the countryside in groups of two. They often went as traveling salesmen offering their wares from door to door. After talking with a resident, they then offered their true merchandise—the Gospel. Taking the pattern from Jesus, at times they even sent out groups of 70 as powerful missionary bands.

Their movement spread into Austria, Bohemia, Moravia, Hungary, Poland, and Spain. Waldo's burden to see the Bible in the common language influenced many reformed groups after him. Eventually, the Waldensians became a threat to the Catholic church, so they, in company with the early Christians, sealed their faith with their lives. Through it all, taking the Sermon on the Mount literally, they loved their enemies, blessed their persecutors, and trusted God for their every provision. Stuart Murray, writing for *Anabaptist Research*, said of their witness for nonresistance:

> "Early Waldensians were committed to nonviolence, deriving this emphasis from a literal reading of the Gospels. They spoke out against violence: crusades against infidels and warfare in general; killing Jews; execution of thieves who were caught stealing food for their families in times of famine; capital punishment; and coercion in matters of faith. This instinctive nonviolence persisted through the centuries."[2]

Czech Brethren

Another pre-reformation group, about A.D. 1420, bravely held to the apostolic faith in the hills of Czechoslovakia. These believers were known as the Czech Brethren. Under the leadership of Peter Chelcicky, this group spoke out strongly in favor of Christian nonresistance. Because of the association of the church mixing with the Empire, Peter Chelcicky boldly declared that the Pope and the Emperor acting as representatives of the church and the state were "whales who have torn the net of true faith."

He taught that no physical power could destroy evil and that Christians should accept persecution without retaliating. Philosophically, he challenged the peasants, teaching them that if the poor refused to go to war, then the rich kings would have no one to fight for them. Specifically to Christians, he taught that they should refuse military service.[3]

In a letter rebuking the idea of so-called "Christian" nations going to war with other "Christian" nations, Peter wrote:

> "The whole rabble of these divided multitudes are called Christians, and together they pray: 'Our Father which art in heaven.' They approach God in this way while each party has in mind the destruction of the other. They think they are serving God by shedding others' blood. And on both sides they say: 'Forgive us as we forgive.' And every party seeks to increase its military force and never thinks of forgiving the other so long as they can hope to overcome them. Therefore, their prayers are blasphemies against God."[4]

Coming on to the Reformation, many Christians came alive with new faith in Jesus Christ and His promises. The Bible was beginning to be taken seriously on a large scale, and accordingly, the world was radically changed.

Erasmus

Even one Catholic scholar, Desiderius Erasmus, attempted to bring reform within the Catholic church. Erasmus was well versed in the original languages of the Scriptures and many of the writings of the early church. As a result, he came out decidedly on the side of nonresistance. He wrote:

> "They who defend war must defend the dispositions which lead to war, and these dispositions are abso-

lutely forbidden by the gospel. Since the time that Jesus Christ said, 'Put up thy sword into its sheath,' Christians ought not to go to war. Christ suffered Peter to fall into an error in this matter, on purpose that, when he had put up Peter's sword, it might remain no longer a doubt that war was prohibited, which before that order had been considered as allowable." [5]

The Anabaptists

Certainly, the most outspoken group of Christians during the time of the Reformation was the Anabaptists. Called by their persecutors, "Anabaptists," which literally means "re-baptizers," modern historians have called this movement "The Radical Reformation." It started around 1530, stemming from the Reformation started by Martin Luther and Ulrich Zwingli. The Anabaptists felt that the early Reformers didn't go far enough, so they endeavored to bring in a restoration of the early church. This meant calling the church to greater levels of radical commitment to Christ.

For many of their noncompromising stands, scores of courageous Anabaptist saints of God were persecuted by the Catholics and Protestants alike. Through it all, however, they were renowned for their supernatural and otherworldly ability to love their enemies, even through the most brutal and merciless treatment their persecutors could inflict. Their powerful testimonies made my petty, uncomfortable situations seem as nothing.

Menno Simons

One very influential early Anabaptist was Menno Simons. Raised a peasant in war-torn Friesland, or modern-day Holland, Menno Simons trained for the priesthood and was ordained a Catholic priest in 1524. By 1526, he was having serious doubts about many doctrines of the church. But his greatest change came about after hearing of an early Anabaptist who was be-headed in 1531 for being re-baptized. The devotion and zeal of these early Anabaptists changed him forever. After Peter Simons (who possibly was his brother) was killed during a religious insurrection in 1535, he finally gave his life completely to Christ, trusting in the efficacy of Jesus' blood. He wrote of this night:

> "My heart trembled in my body. I prayed to God with sighs and tears, that he would give to me, a troubled sinner, the gift of his grace, and create a clean heart within me; that through the merits of the crimson blood of Christ, He would graciously forgive my unclean walk and unprofitable life, and bestow upon me, wisdom, Spirit, candor and fortitude, that I might preach his exalted and adorable name and holy word unperverted, and make manifest his truth to his praise."[6]

Following his conversion in 1536, he left the priesthood and joined the Anabaptists.[7] Writing about war, Menno Simons said:

> "The regenerated do not go to war, nor engage in strife. They are the children of peace who

have beaten their swords into plowshares and their spears into pruning hooks, and know of no war. They render unto Caesar the things that are Caesar's and unto God the things that are God's. Their sword is the sword of the Spirit which they wield with a good conscience through the Holy Ghost."[8]

"Our weapons are not weapons with which cities and countries may be destroyed, walls and gates broken down, and human blood shed in torrents like water. But they are weapons with which the spiritual kingdom of the devil is destroyed... Christ is our fortress; patience our weapon of defense; the Word of God our sword. And our victory is a candid, firm, unfeigned faith in Jesus Christ. Iron and metal spears and swords we leave to those who, alas, regard human blood and swine's blood of well-nigh equal value."[9]

Jacob Hutter

On the other side of Europe, in modern day Italy, Jacob Hutter led many believers to a radical walking out of the Sermon on the Mount. Their missionary zeal to share their faith spread quickly across Europe. Literally thousands were baptized upon profession of their faith as adults, although to do so meant they had committed a crime punishable by death. After a time of persecution they ended up in Moravia (present-day Czech Republic) where religious toleration was granted to them.

In 1535, a bounty equal to a soldier's yearly wage

was placed on Jacob Hutter's head. In November of 1535, after returning from a missionary trip to Tirol, northern Italy, in an attempt to bring people back with him, he and his wife were captured. After condemning him to death, the authorities tried to bargain with him to secure names of other believers. But he gave them none. To make an example of him, the emperor of the Holy Roman Empire, Ferdinand I, had him severely whipped, placed on the rack, and tortured. In February 1536, Ferdinand had him taken to the city square of Innsbruck, Austria, held in freezing water, then placed in a hot room. Brandy then was poured into his wounds. After this torture, he was taken to the city square and publicly burned at the stake. All along, he never denied the faith or turned in his fellow believers.

During his life, Jacob Hutter spoke out strongly against Christians in warfare. Speaking of the true Christians he wrote:

> "We will not do a wrong or an injury to any man, yea, not to our greatest enemy, neither to Ferdinand, nor anyone else, great or small. All our actions and conduct, word and work, life and walk are open; there is no secret about it all. Rather than knowingly to rob a man of a penny, we would willingly give up a hundred guilders. And before we would give our greatest enemy a blow with the hand, to say nothing of spear, sword, or halberd as is the manner of the world, we would be willing to lose our lives."[10]

More Groups

As I read, I continued to discover more and more

groups who, after taking the Bible seriously, ended up with many of the same convictions. For example there were the "Brethren" groups under the leadership of men such as Peter Becker and Alexander Mack. They too continued to call the church to return to apostolic Christianity.

In 1785, the Church of the Brethren stated in their Annual Conference that they should not "submit to the higher powers so as to make ourselves their instruments to shed human blood...The church cannot concede to the state the authority to conscript citizens for military training or military service against their conscience." Even today, their descendents—the German Baptists, the Dunkard Brethren, and the church of the Brethren—still hold to these teachings.

Early Methodists

It seemed that whenever groups of Christians gathered together and covenanted to take the Bible seriously, this doctrine of nonresistance naturally came out. Even some of the early Methodist circuit riders, filled with the Holy Spirit and anointed preaching, could not resist the clear teaching of Jesus on this subject. John Nelson, the first person to offer his services as a lay preacher to John Wesley, was at one time taken by force, clothed in a uniform, and with rifle forced into his hand told that he was to stay in uniform and fight. He boldly told these military commanders that he would wear the uniform as a cross, but he would not fight.

Two of the most influential early Methodists, Barbara Heck and her husband Paul, refused to support the Revolutionary War. This conviction cost them great financial loss. At one time, they were stopped by a British officer, who tried to compel Paul to join the Army to defend the king. To this, Paul Heck replied "I have taken service under the best kings, and I desire no better. And as for King George, God bless him. I am willing to suffer in body and estate for his cause, but I cannot fight. I would ever hear the voice of the master whom I serve, saying, 'Put up thy sword in its sheath.'"

Early Methodist leader, Jesse Lee, speaking briefly but thoughtfully on the subject wrote, "I weighed the matter over and over again, but my mind was settled as a Christian, and as a preacher I could not fight."[11]

The Martyrs Mirror—Dirk Willems

All these testimonies dramatically affected me, but per-haps the most impressive story of nonresistance and Christlike faith recorded during these troubling times was that of Dirk Willems. I was amazed when I read his story as recorded in the *Martyrs Mirror*.

The Martyrs Mirror was compiled by Thieleman J. Van Braght in 1660. This book exhaustively goes through each age of the church, detailing the testimon-ies of brave men, women, and children who gave their lives for their faith in Jesus Christ. Most of the focus centers on the persecuted church during the time of the Radical Reformation.

Dirk Willems was a young man who converted to Christianity in Holland during a time of great persecu-tion. The Spanish had ruled Holland and, wanting to stabilize the country, they tried to stamp out the Anabaptists and other radical Christian nonconformists. Apparently, Dirk was no quiet believer, but instead, shared his faith openly and even allowed others to be baptized in his home. Dirk, after being arrested, was tried and committed to prison for his faith.

After he had been in for some time, Dirk figured a way of escape. Taking bed sheets and tying knots in them, he let himself down the prison walls. Unfortunately, he was quickly spotted by the burgomaster, and a deputy was sent immediately in pursuit. Dirk swiftly made his escape over a body of thin ice.

I imagine Dirk must have thought for a moment that he might just pull this off. However, the much heavier deputy also attempted to cross the thin ice. But to his peril, the ice gave way and the deputy fell through the ice and would have drowned. Dirk was well on his way when he heard his pursuer's cry for rescue. Turning around, he realized that the deputy had fallen into the ice and was now pleading for his life.

I have often wondered what Dirk Willems must have been thinking at that moment. In front of him was his life—his freedom. All he had to do was keep running. Who would blame him if he didn't turn around to aid the deputy? He had been falsely imprisoned, and to return now would inevitably cost him his life. But Dirk had died to himself years before when he gave his life to Christ. Now, if any real temptations to keep going raced through his mind at this moment, we would never know it from this account.

Jesus taught that His followers must love their enemies, feed them, and even bless them. Dirk knew that Jesus had done that very thing for him, and now it was his turn to do the same for this drowning man. So Dirk immediately turned around and pulled his pursuer out of the ice.

The deputy was greatly moved by this unprecedented act of compassion and wanted to let Dirk go free. However, looking on from a distance, the burgomaster screamed to the deputy, reminding him that he had sworn an oath of loyalty. Sadly, the burgomaster persuaded the deputy to choose loyalty to the state over compassion for his rescuer, so the deputy apprehended Dirk and brought him back into captivity.

Once back in captivity, his persecutors showed him no compassion for his act of mercy. Instead, they re-convicted him for his crime of heresy and rebaptism. The report says that he then was placed in severe imprisonment until the day that he finally was taken to the city square to be burned at the stake. His was an awful death.

The eyewitness reports say that a strong east wind was blowing, and that the upper part of the fire was being blown away, leaving Dirk to suffer horribly because only the lower portion of the fire was burning him. The eyewitnesses said that they heard him cry out "O my Lord, my God!" more than 70 times. Finally, a local official traveling by on horseback was filled with sorrow for the young man. He ordered that the fire be arranged so that Dirk would die quickly.

The Martyrs Mirror finishes its epitaph on Dirk Willems' life saying:

> "But as he had founded his faith not upon the drifting sand of human commandments, but upon the firm foundation stone, Christ Jesus, he, notwithstanding all evil winds of human doctrine, and heavy showers of tyrannical and severe persecution, remained immovable and steadfast unto the end; wherefore, when the

chief Shepherd shall appear in the clouds of heaven and gather together His elect from all the ends of the earth, he shall also through grace hear the words, 'Well done, good and faithful servant; thou hast been faithful over a few things, I will make thee ruler over many things; enter thou into the joy of thy Lord.'"[12]

I thought, "Oh, that I might have a testimony just like that! A testimony of a life undoubtedly sold out to God, so that when all is said and done, I too might run confidently into the welcoming arms of our blessed Savior and hear that glorious salutation, 'Enter thou into the joy of thy Lord!'"

After saturating ourselves in stories of saints such as these, Tania and I no longer felt alone. We felt encouraged. We felt welcomed. We still felt like sojourners, but in the midst of the pilgrimage, we felt at home. Hebrews 12 became dear to us:

"Therefore we also, since we are surrounded by so great a cloud of witnesses, let us lay aside every weight, and the sin which so easily ensnares us, and let us run with endurance the race that is set before us, looking unto Jesus, the author and finisher of our faith."[13]

Chapter Ten
The Two Kingdoms

Swearing in the second time

With her back turned to me, shuffling through some paperwork, the staff psychologist said with an obvious touch of challenge in her voice, "Come on in...but I really don't think you will be in here long enough to even need to sit down."

Standing there a bit awkwardly, I probed, "What do you mean...I don't understand."

This was supposed to be a very routine interview. Every person who submits a request for conscientious objector discharge in the military has to go through several prearranged hurdles. All applicants must submit their request to their commander, have an interview with the base chaplain, be interviewed by a psychologist, prepare a lengthy report answering the military's standard questions, and survive a court hearing in which just about any questions can be asked. Once this is completed, a portfolio of the resulting information is sent to the Pentagon for approval.

Of all of these interviews, from my understanding, the one with the psychologist was merely supposed to assess whether the "disturbed" applicant was mentally able to stand trial. I didn't think this interview was going to be antagonistic at all—but I was wrong. From her very first words, I could tell that this was going to be a challenge. After I asked her what she meant by her stark introduction, she finally looked at me and said...

"I've got you!"

"What do you mean 'you've got me?'" I asked as I slowly grabbed my chair and sat down.

"I've got you figured out." Looking upset, she stared me right in the eye and said, "You're inconsistent."

"I'm inconsistent? What do you mean?"

"All of you conscientious objectors are inconsistent.

There was a group of you in here last week, and I saw right through your arguments. You're inconsistent—you all are inconsistent."

Trembling a bit, I tried to act brave and said, "Okay, so how are we inconsistent?"

"It's easy," she said, putting her chair squarely in my direction behind her desk. Then she said condescendingly, "Okay, you say you want out of the Army because you feel that you cannot conscientiously support the Army. Is that correct?"

"Yes ma'am."

"Okay, I'll ask you another question."

"Alright."

"Do you believe in paying your taxes?"

"Well, yes ma'am, I do."

Throwing herself back in her chair, she said with a slight condescending laugh, "You see—I've got you! You're inconsistent!" After she spoke, she sat back in her chair as if this would end the discussion.

I wasn't completely sure how to answer her in a way she would understand. Instead of using human reasoning, my desire was to point her to God's Word. I leaned forward in my chair, took a deep breath and said, "Ma'am, you may not understand this, but…you see, I live by the standards of a book, and that book is the Bible. This Bible tells me to love my enemies and to pay my taxes. I don't have to understand it, I just have to obey it."

Things quickly went downhill from there. The psychologist became very upset and a bit irrational with several arguments that followed. When I told her I wanted to be like Jesus, she snipped, "Nowhere in the Bible does it say that we are to be like Jesus!"

When I began to offer her a scripture about walking in His steps and having the mind of Christ, she abruptly cut me off and said, "Listen, you don't need to preach to me. I know the Bible."

At this point, she was looking very severe. She continued, "I know the Bible very well. Do you *realize* what I have done?" She then listed off a long list of charities, volunteer activities, Bible study groups that she had led, and the like. Then she capped it all off with the rather strange statement, "And besides all of that, I'll have you know I am a card-carrying Methodist!"

What was I to say? I began to feel a bit sorry for her. She had lost her professional composure. I now admit that what I said next probably was a bit contentious.

I looked at her and replied, waving my hand, "Could you please just repeat all of that?"

"All of what?"

"All of those accomplishments."

She continued her monologue, and then dismissed me after asking me if I was hard of hearing.

The Two Kingdoms

Thinking about the interview, I realized that the psychologist had unwittingly hit on a very fundamental dividing line in the understanding of Christian nonresistance. That dividing line is the understanding that there are two kingdoms.

The teaching of the two kingdoms presents the spiritual reality that the children of God, while still living here on earth, are governed by a heavenly kingdom ruled and dictated by God. It proclaims that when Jesus came to earth, He established this kingdom. Furthermore, this kingdom transcends all nations, tribes, languages, geography, and time. And although this kingdom is spiritually discerned, it is lived out practically in the real world.

However, unlike God's Kingdom in the Old Testament, with one geographic area representing God's Kingdom, the Kingdom of God described in the New Testament has been dispersed throughout all nations. As salt and light to the world, the people of God are led by a different law and a different constitution. Ultimately, as citizens, they take their orders from a different king.

Caesar or God

Perhaps the most well-known and often misquoted passage concerning the idea of the two kingdoms and our relationship with earthly kings is the passage from Matthew 22. The Pharisees in this account tried to tempt Jesus in the matter of paying taxes to Caesar. It is here that Jesus replied, "Render therefore unto Caesar the things which are Caesar's; and unto God the things that are God's."[1]

Most Christians believe in a two-kingdom concept in some form. The differences come in deciding which things belong to Caesar and which belong to God. As I continued to study the Bible and the early church, I noticed that the early Christians drew that line with a decisive stroke. The Apostle Peter spoke to Christians as if they did not belong to the earthly kingdoms in which they lived. He referred to these early believers as sojourners, as aliens, or as pilgrims: "And if ye call on the Father, who without respect of persons judgeth according to every man's work, pass the time of your sojourning here in fear" (1 Peter 1:17).

God's heart throughout the whole Bible is for His people to be satiated with His presence. The book of Acts is a living example of God's people governed, led, taught, and directed by His presence. The New Testament Christians respected the governments under which they lived. However, they paid their foremost allegiance to God. As Peter and John said before their judges in Acts 4:19, "Whether it is right in the sight of God to listen to you more than to God, you judge." This was a bold stance, but it was this stance that "turned the world upsidedown."[2]

When I considered the condition of the church when these lines began to fade, it became obvious to me that both the church and the world became the losers. The world lost its salt and light; the church lost its purpose.

My Kingdom Is Not of This World

The line between the two kingdoms is graphically demonstrated shortly before the crucifixion when Jesus stood before Pontius Pilate. Pilate had heard that people were calling Jesus a king, so he challenged Jesus: "Are You the King of the Jews?"[3]

Jesus took these words seriously and answered back: "Are you speaking for yourself about this, or did others tell you this concerning Me?"[4]

Pilate snapped back "Am I a Jew? Your own nation and the chief priests have delivered You to me. What have You done?"[5]

At this statement Jesus made a decisive announcement. Looking past all time, place, philosophies, and nations Jesus replied: "My kingdom is not of this world."[6]

Immediately following this proclamation, Jesus described the marching orders of His people: "If My kingdom were of this world, My servants would fight, so that I should not be delivered to the Jews; but now My kingdom is not from here."[7]

Pilate then answered Jesus like so many of us today, by interpreting Jesus' words as merely figurative, mystical jargon or spiritual talk. He asked, "Are You a king then?"[8]

That's just the way I used to look at God's kingdom. I knew that Jesus spoke of a kingdom, but I didn't *really* think that His kingdom was to be lived out in practical ways. However, Jesus' answer is corrective and astounding. With no hint of confusion, weakness or compromise, Jesus replied: "You say rightly that I am a king. For this cause I was born."[9]

That last statement still makes me stop and think. Apparently the idea of being a king was no minor point to Jesus. Jesus said that He was born for this very reason—to be a king!

Jesus finished His declaration saying "And for this cause I have come into the world, that I should bear witness to the truth. Everyone who is of the truth hears My voice."[10]

I saw that this showdown between Jesus and Pilate was a decided pronouncement of the priority, reality, and importance of the Kingdom of God.

No Fraternization With the Enemy

Paul cautioned the young minister Timothy to keep a clear understanding of our place among the nations. He told Timothy that the Christian should see himself as a loyal, determined soldier in the army of God, not distracted by concerns outside his domain. He reminded Timothy that such a soldier does not have the time, or even the right to involve himself in the affairs of countries he was providentially intended to occupy: "You therefore must endure hardship as a good soldier of Jesus Christ. No one engaged in warfare entangles himself with the affairs of this life, that he may please him who enlisted him as a soldier."[11]

A Man in Uniform

As an American soldier in a foreign country, this analogy came alive to me. At that time, Tania and I were American citizens living in Germany on a military assignment. We lived in a German-owned apartment, had German utilities, and paid for them both with German currency. We might have known who the German President was at that time, but if we did, it was only by chance. We certainly were not allowed to vote in their elections, nor would we have even desired to do so. We wore the American uniform, spoke American English, and paid American income taxes. At that time, we even watched American television and voted in American elections. It simply would not have been acceptable for me to run for office as the local burgomaster or hope for a seat in the German Parliament. We had no place in their armies or their politics. We were

American soldiers, and we knew we had a job to do.

Likewise, in the Kingdom of God, clarity in our vocation provides distinction in our behavior. When the line between the two kingdoms became clearer to me, I recognized many things in my life as blatant fraternization with the occupied country. The more my wife and I made decisions based on scriptural doctrine and precedent, the more we found ourselves as aliens and sojourners, even among our own countrymen. I found that the more distinctly the line between the two kingdoms was drawn, the clearer all the teachings of Christ became. To confuse these contrasting kingdoms made nonsense out of the teachings of Christ.

It is notable that even a man like Adolph Hitler understood that a true Christian's loyalty could not be intimately entrusted to the state. He complained that loyalty would be compromised if a man's allegiance was divided—"One is either a good German or a good Christian. It is impossible to be both at the same time."[12]

Caesar or God

This dichotomy of living *in* the world but not *of* the world, however, poses a continual tension.

- **If** we have our own laws that rule and govern our lives—(Luke 6:46; Matt 7:21–27; 1 John 5:3; 2 John 6)
- **If** we have our own king that demands absolute loyalty—(Zech 9:9; John 19:14; Rev 17:14)
- **If** we are to refuse to obey laws that contradict the Laws of God—(Matt 5:28; Acts 5:29)
- **If** we are to love, feed, warm, and care, even for

the enemies of the countries in which we live—(Matt 5:44; Rom 12:20)

- **If** we are charged with the impractical marching orders of going forth as lambs before wolves, or sheep before the slaughter—(Luke 10:3; Rom 8:36)
- **If** our weapons are not made of earthly things—(Eph 6:12)
- **If** we do not war "in the flesh"—(2 Cor 10:3–7)
- **If** we understand that, in contrast to the Old Testament marching orders to destroy men's lives, we now instead have orders to save them—(Luke 9:51–56)
- **If** dying actually is gain for us, and the cross our example—(Phil 1:21; I Cor 1:18)
- **If** our kingdom is not of this world—(John 18:3)
- **If** in the end, we defeat even the antichrist, only by the blood of the Lamb, the word of our testimony, and not loving our lives, even unto death—(Rev 12:11)

Then—how must we respond to all of these earthly kings and rulers? What do we do with the hundreds of laws and ordinances that affect so much of our life? What allegiance do we owe to the kings and empires that have spread around the world and throughout time? Embracing a two-kingdom worldview places new challenges for us concerning what we should do with the worldly kingdom. The temptation to ignore their bothersome rules and ridiculous bureaucracies is strong. I was tempted to ask the question, "Should I even bother with their laws and government?"

Chapter Eleven
Romans 13

I saw that Romans 13 provided an effective touchstone to reveal just how clear the line was between the two kingdoms in my life. This chapter tests those who make claims to biblical nonresistance. Certainly, belittling the government, destructive protesting, and anti-authority rhetoric generally finds itself out of place in this chapter. But how should I view these earthly rulers? Could I deny the fact that God has raised up armies, kings, and powerful men to put an end to such atrocities as communism, Nazism, and countless tyrants throughout the ages? If I admitted to myself that God has indeed used armies and men such as this to accomplish His will, does this mean that God's blessing was on these people?

These questions perplexed me, particularly when I weighed the arguments of both sides. On the one hand, the religious conservatives were trying to tell me that America was God's country, so I should embrace the agenda of the government. Any self-respecting Christian conservative worth his salt would quickly take me to Romans 13. On the other hand, the liberal writers were attempting to advocate some kind of political-pacifist-ecumenical, new utopian government (or "global community," as they might call it). As I studied and searched the Scriptures, I found Romans 13 to be the dividing line that distinguishes genuine, biblical, two-kingdom theology. Here is the text:

> "Let every soul be subject to the governing authorities. For there is no authority except from God, and the authorities that exist are *appointed by God*. Therefore whoever resists the authority resists the ordinance of God, and those who resist will bring judgment on themselves. For rulers are not a

terror to good works, but to evil. Do you want to be unafraid of the authority? Do what is good, and you will have praise from the same. For he is *God's minister* to you for good. But if you do evil, be afraid; for he does not *bear the sword in vain*; for he is God's minister, an avenger to execute wrath on him who practices evil. Therefore you must be subject, not only because of wrath but also for con- science' sake."[1]

In this passage, often quoted by my politically con- servative friends, the role of earthly government is said to be "ordained of God." What's more, this passage even calls these rulers "the ministers of God." My friends would often point out that these ministers "bear not the sword in vain." These are strong words! I wondered how I was ever going to balance these words with the command of Jesus to "love your enemies."

Ministers of God

I struggled with this in thought and prayer for some time. I began to read and ask people to explain these verses further to me. I finally got up the nerve to talk to the owner of the local Christian book store, who was also a pastor. I told him about my growing convictions for nonresistance, and he stuffed a video in my hand about a Christian policeman. The policeman in this video was questioning his responsibility if called on to kill people in the line of duty. The movie, basing its claim on Romans 13, explained that this man was a "minister of God." It went on to argue that there were no inconsistencies in the Christian policeman having to kill in this setting because the whole thing was ordained of God. Furthermore, it reasoned that if it is ordained of God, then it must also, therefore, be blessed of God.

But this is where I saw the difference. I asked, "Does being ordained of God also guarantee that something is blessed of God?" Finally, I concluded that it did not. Profoundly, I found this difference unequivocally demonstrated in the life of Jesus.

The Authority to Crucify Jesus

Once again, I considered the scene when Jesus was before Pontius Pilate. After Jesus' proclamation of His Kingdom, Pilate had Jesus beaten and his soldiers forced a crown of thorns on Jesus' head and mocked Him, putting a purple robe on Him saying, "Hail, King of the Jews!"[2] Pilate declared Jesus' innocence as he brought Jesus before the crowd: "Then Jesus came out, wearing the crown of thorns and the purple robe. And Pilate said to them, 'Behold the Man!' Therefore, when the chief priests and officers saw Him, they cried out, saying, 'Crucify Him, crucify Him!'"[3]

There Jesus stood, the ultimate Authority, the King of kings, the Creator of the universe. Bruised, humiliated, beaten, and exhausted, he was shamed before what appeared to be a superior authority over Him. Pilate gallantly boasted his perceived power and authority over Jesus stating, "Are You not speaking to me? Do You not know that I have power to crucify You, and power to release You?"[4]

I thought long and hard over those words. Here Pilate said, "I have power to crucify You, and power to release You."

Was this true? Did Pilate really have this power?

To this affirmation, Jesus responded in words that still amaze me each time I read them: "Jesus answered, 'You could have no power at all against Me unless it had been given you from above.'"[5]

This declaration implied that Jesus had the ability not only to set himself free, but also that He could, at any time, put an end to Pilate's trifling little domain in a moment.

But this I knew. I knew that God was more powerful than any human authority. He had demonstrated this kind of power all through the Bible. To me the most profound thing about this passage was not the proclamation of God's ultimate power over earthly kingdoms, but the quintessential thought—the very idea of Jesus being there in that situation before Pilate in the first place.

There before Pilate, Jesus indicated that although it is true that the ultimate authority over this situation was indeed according to the Father's power and will, it also is true—as inconceivable as it may seem—that Pilate, at this time, was given the power and authority to crucify Him! I saw clearly that even though this act was within God's ultimate will, God obviously did not *bless* Pilate or the centurions for performing it. With this distinction, the role of human government in general became much clearer to me.

When Paul called the ruler the "minister of God" in Romans 13, I found it instructive to remember just *who* this ruler was. In Paul's day, it was not a liberal American Baptist from Arkansas, or even a conservative Evangelical from Texas. In Paul's day, this "minister of God," depending on when you date the Epistle, was either Caligula or Nero. In either case, the ruler was one of the most wicked figures in the history of the church. Why?

Why?

I believe Paul called him the "minister of God" because Paul clearly understood the Emperor's place was in this worldly kingdom, and that Paul's place was in another kingdom—the Kingdom of God.

In the previous chapter (Romans 12), Paul exhorted the church at Rome not to be conformed to the ways of the world. Elaborating on this, he discussed the need for humility, self-denial, not taking revenge, not rendering evil for evil, and even feeding our enemies. He concluded the chapter with these words: "Be not overcome with evil, but overcome evil with good."

With such an indictment against the ways of the world, if we are not careful, we could easily deduce that Christians are above the law. Irritating things such as taxes, customs, bureaucracies, civil honors, and menacing laws can seem beneath the Christian, who is a citizen of such a glorious kingdom from above. However, against this mindset, Paul instructs the church to be obedient down to the smallest detail.

> "Therefore you must be subject, not only because of wrath but also for conscience' sake. For because of this you also pay taxes, for they are *God's ministers* attending continually to this very thing. Render therefore to all their due: taxes to whom taxes are due, customs to whom customs, fear to whom fear, honor to whom honor."[6]

I clearly saw that respect, honor, and all the possible obedience I could give should be rendered to my rulers and earthly authorities. However, to enter their kingdom, to take up their causes, their wars, and their weapons was clearly disallowed. Respect was one thing, but to jump from a teaching on civil responsibility and honor to a total abandonment of the teaching of Jesus was simply illogical, out of context, and perhaps even dishonest.

Old Testament "Ministers"

As I studied the Bible, I saw that God actually had always used kings and countries as servants or "ministers" to accomplish His will, even throughout the Old Testament. What's more, I found that in the history of Israel, even though God used a king as "His minister," God also showed that He certainly did not mean that the king was blessed by Him in any real sense.

The book of Jeremiah records a striking example of a king outside God's Kingdom being used by God to punish His own people. Significantly, Jeremiah reveals how God felt about them all along. The setting is the time right before Judah was carried off to exile in Babylon for 70 years. Judah had continually abandoned God's covenant, and now God was going to use the king of Babylon to execute judgment on God's own people:

> "Therefore thus says the LORD of hosts: 'Because you have not heard My words, behold, I will send and take all the families of the north,' says the LORD, 'and Nebuchadnezzar the king of Babylon, *My servant*, and will bring them

against this land, against its inhabitants, and against these nations all around, and will utterly destroy them, and make them an astonishment, a hissing, and perpetual desolations.'"[7]

Notice the words "My servant." This Hebrew terminology is the equivalent of the word Paul uses in Romans 13 about earthly rulers such as Nero. The word "minister" used in Romans 13 is taken from the Greek word "diakonos." This word literally means "servant." It is from this word that we get our English word for deacon. In both the Old and the New Testaments, God used pagan, idol-worshiping kings to execute His purposes, even calling them "My servant"—or rather, "My minister."

Ordained of God Does Not Necessarily Mean Blessed of God

But again, how should I think about these kings? If they are "ordained of God," should I conclude that they also are "blessed of God" and align myself with them? Just three verses later, God reveals exactly how He felt about this king and this kingdom that He used to accomplish His will:

> "Then it will come to pass, when seventy years are completed, that I will punish the king of Babylon and that nation, the land of the Chaldeans, for their iniquity," says the LORD; "and I will make it a perpetual desolation."[8]

I saw that Israel's obedience to Nebuchadnezzar was necessary, but to align themselves with Babylon would have been a big mistake.

Also, there was the prophecy of Isaiah about the pagan king, Cyrus, who was strategically used in the capture of Babylon by damming up the Euphrates River. God called him "my shepherd."[9] This did not mean that God was pleased with Cyrus' pagan idolatry. It meant only that Cyrus was used by God as a "shepherd" to do His will.

America

So what about me? Could I admit that God has used America and other countries like her throughout time to accomplish His goals? Absolutely. But I could see that to take this fact and allow myself subtly to be led to believe that the Kingdom of God and the kingdom of the earth are somehow joined would also be a big mistake.

Tertullian, speaking about A.D. 190 on these issues, said:

> "Now inquiry is made about the point of whether a believer may enter into military service. The question is also asked whether those in the military may be admitted into the faith—even the rank and file (or any inferior grade), who are not required to take part in sacrifices or capital punishments...A man cannot give his allegiance to two masters—God and Caesar."[10]

The Price of Compromise

Interestingly, yet tragically, during World War II when the world trembled under the threat of Adolph Hitler and his tyrannical reign of power and genocidal holocaust, millions of Americans, including millions of

"American Christians," decided that to strengthen themselves against Hitler, they would form a league with Joseph Stalin. Later, historical accounts revealed that Joseph Stalin was responsible quite possibly for as many as three times as many deaths as Hitler. Again, the words of Paul come to mind, "Be not overcome with evil, but overcome evil with good."[11]

It became clear to me that as far as the affairs of the earthly kingdom were concerned, God does not desire disorder and anarchy. Instead, He ensures that each nation will be ordered, legislated, and governed. As God said through Jeremiah concerning God's decision to use Babylon for his purposes:

> "I have made the earth, the man and the beast that are on the ground, by My great power and by My outstretched arm, and have given it to whom it seemed proper to Me. And now I have given all these lands into the hand of Nebuchadnezzar the king of Babylon, My servant; and the beasts of the field I have also given him to serve him."[12]

The prophet Daniel proclaimed this fact to all the angels and inhabitants of the earth. He even added an humbling insight into how God actually looks at these kings:

> "This decision is by the decree of the watchers, And the sentence by the word of the holy ones, In order that the living may know That the Most High rules in the kingdom of men, Gives it to whomever He will, And sets over it the lowest of men."[13]

Or, as Solomon poetically put it:

> "The king's heart is in the hand of the LORD,
> Like the rivers of water; He turns it wherever
> He wishes."[14]

The difference between "ordained of God" and "blessed of God" became distinct to me. In obedience to God, I am to obey my authorities, pay my taxes, and submit to their laws so long as they do not contradict God's laws. However, all along, I must realize that this kingdom is not my home. My identity, my goal, and my agenda is to be in Christ and His Kingdom.

Chapter Twelve
My Defender Is God

A tired me at basic training

When I was an 11-year-old in sixth grade, I had a good friend named Ricky Luna. He was a bit clumsy and awkward, and I suppose he didn't look as "cool" as some of the more popular children in our school. Similarly, I was tall, clumsy, and overly confident. My school, Grace Harding Elementary, was the typical worldly, semi-suburban, public elementary school. It had your usual cliques: athletic, musical, cowboy, preppie, druggy, and so on. These subgroups had a big effect on who your friends were and how you were going to be treated by the other children of your class.

Ricky and I signed up for band, and because of this, we found ourselves quickly herded into the less-than-popular "band-geeks" subgroup. This juvenile caste system immediately put us with the "untouchables," oftentimes turning the playground and walks home into times of taunting and feuds.

Well, Ricky had it even worse than I did. Toting his brand new 'Bundy' alto saxophone, sporting his strangely uncut and quite unfashionable hair, his gleaming silver-laced grin, hunched shoulders, and an uncoordinated gait—all juxtaposed with a name like "Luna,"—made him a trophy in the bullying and harassment game. But he was my friend.

One afternoon as we began our daily mission and maneuvers to walk home unscathed, we were met by one of the chief taunters, Frankie Jones. He started the usual cadence, "Luna is a tu-na...Luna is a tu-na!"

I, reminiscent of my Davie Crockett chivalry, demanded that he "leave Ricky alone." To my surprise, he backed off, and we left in peace. I thought, "Wow! He was scared of me!" Ricky thanked me, and I felt as tough as a bulldog puppy after winning a battle by biting his littermate's ear. I even told my parents when I got home, and they seemed proud of me. This all made it clear to me—strength wins. I came to understand that brawn, confidence, and wit would be what I needed to make it through hard situations like this.

A couple of months later, however, I learned that I was wrong. On our march home from school, we were headed for Ricky's house. When we were about half-way there, in a construction area for some new homes, we met Frankie Jones again. This time he ran up, pushed Ricky's shoulder, and started the familiar croon, "Luna is a tu-na...Luna is a tu-na...Luna is a tu-na!" This time I was ready. Equipped with the assurance of past victories, I demanded that he stop, and "just leave Ricky alone!"

"Who's gonna' stop me?" he challenged.

"I am!" I said, as I dropped my school books and slide-trombone.

Pushing my shoulder, he challenged, "You wanna fight!"

"Yea!" And I put up my skinny fist.

Now, I had never been in a fight quite like this before. Sure, I had been beat up by my older brother a few hundred times, but even in that, we always had a determined sense of reserve not to leave marks or draw blood. We both knew if either one of us *really* got hurt, the beating we would get later from Dad would be worse.

This wasn't the case now. Suddenly, this big, strapping 11-year-old boy was shifting and ducking around me like Rocky Balboa. The alarm from the onlookers went out—"Fight!" Out of nowhere came a crowd of spectators, transforming this unfriendly squabble at a construction site into a Las Vegas-style heavyweight boxing tournament. The crowd jeered, "Hit 'em!", "Come-on, fight!", "Do something!"

Then it happened...Frankie acted like he was going to hit me with his left fist, so I threw up a block. But as my attention was diverted to this punch, he was wrenching his body over and reaching way back and suddenly...

Smack!!!!

With all Frankie's might, his big right fist connected under my left eye. Suddenly, everything went black and down I went, hitting the ground. As I came to, I saw Frankie standing over me yelling to his friend, "Hey, it worked," as if they were practicing some kind of box-ing moves. I then looked to the crowd, and they were all still screaming:

"Hit 'em!"

"Hit 'em again!"

"Hit 'em while he's down!"

I started to cry, and Frankie looked to the crowd and told them he could not hit me while I was crying. He then looked at me and challenged me with something like

"Had enough wimp?"

I whimpered out a "yes," and he left me alone.

He walked away followed by a parade of cheers from his admiring public. Ricky and I hardly said a word to each other. I went to his house for awhile, then later I started my approximate three-mile walk to my house. Once home, in full Norman Rockwell fashion, my mother placed a steak on my eye and my father inquisitively asked, "So what does the other guy look like?"

School was embarrassing. If the taunting was bad before, now, sporting my "class A" shiner, I was everyone's target. Once, at the water fountain, Frankie thought he would ensure his ascendancy and ordered me to move or he would "complete my face lift, making me look like a raccoon." Demoralized, I just walked away. I was now the defeated. I saw that might and strength could not stop this foe. I wasn't a Christian yet, but something from within me cried to God for defense. I could not do it myself, and even if I felt it was ridiculous, I knew that what I really needed was an omnipotent defender.

Last Day of Sixth Grade

It was now the last day of school, and not only that; it was the last day in this school building. After this year, we would all move on to different junior high schools according to our local addresses. On this last day, the school had an annual picnic in which the whole sixth grade class walked about two miles to the park.

A few weeks before this, Ricky had shown me a strange little device he said he was carrying around to defend himself from stray dogs. I knew he didn't really care about the dogs, so I challenged him.

"What is that?" I asked.

"It's called mace. You spray it at an attacking dog, and it really burns the dog's eyes bad! After that, the dog will just run away and leave you alone."

"Sounds pretty mean," I challenged.

"No, it doesn't hurt them permanently—just burns real bad at first."

I still wasn't comfortable with the idea, but I soon forgot about it.

Walk to the Park

As we walked to the park, we endured a few tauntings from Frankie and the other bullies, and we wondered what the playground front lines would be like today. Pranks and tricks were common, and we were fearful that some joke might be played on us. So, putting our towels, lunches, and other belongings on the picnic tables, Ricky and I went to the far side of the park to play.

A few hours later, we heard quite a commotion coming from the tables and we wondered what in the world had happened. It wasn't long until Mr. Sharps, our homeroom teacher, was calling for us with a pretty severe tone. We ran to see what the problem was, and there he was holding Ricky's mace spray in his hand.

Looking at us with wrinkled brow and tight lips, he stood there with Ricky's mace in his hand and asked, "What's this?"

Ricky's voice quivered as he squeaked out his reply, "It's a mace squirter, Mr. Sharps."

Holding it out to Ricky, Mr. Sharps asked, "Why do you have a mace squirter?"

"My mom wanted me to have it to scare off the stray dogs. Sometimes they attack me when I'm walking home. But why do you ask? I had it put up. It was hidden. What happened?"

Suddenly, Mr. Sharps' face sobered as he began to tell us what had happened. "Well, apparently," he said motioning with his hand, "Frankie was messing with you boys' personal belongings. I reckon he was intending to do something mischievous. Anyway, I guess while he was messing with Ricky's towel this mace squirter came rolling out. Inspecting it and staring right down the barrel of the squirter, he shot the thing right into his eyes. He then started crying and screaming. It sounded awful! So we took him to the hospital. He'll be okay, but it sure did hurt 'em."

Ricky and I were dumbfounded. I slowly looked over to him; he slowly looked over to me, and then we both looked up to Mr. Sharps, wondering how much trouble we were going to be in for this one. At that point I saw it…Yes, it was there…just to the far left side of his pursed-lip frown was an ever-so-slightly twisted wry grin! Then with a little sparkle in his eyes, he told us to run along and play. "And don't bring that thing around here anymore!"

Now, I obviously had a long way to go in learning how to be a peacemaker. The whole fight-thing could have been avoided had I learned the way of Christ earlier on. But somehow this little incident tucked away in my memory came back to me and taught me a lesson. Retributive justice, just desserts, poetic justice—people have all kinds of names for stuff like this. But I knew then, even as an eleven-year-old, way down deep, that my deliverance was the work of an omnipotent defender.

My Defender

Now, in the Army, as I began to consider the idea of looking only to God as my defender in a real and practical way, this memory came to mind. I pondered this as I read over the Apostle Paul's teaching to the Romans:

> "Repay no one evil for evil. Have regard for good things in the sight of all men. If it is possible, as much as depends on you, live peaceably with all men. Beloved, do not avenge yourselves, but rather give place to wrath; *for it is written, "Vengeance is Mine, I will repay*," says the Lord. Therefore 'If your enemy is hungry, feed him; If he is thirsty, give him a drink; For in so doing you will heap coals of fire on his head.' Do not be overcome by evil, but overcome evil with good."[1]

Later, when my wife and I visited the concentration camps in Germany, we had already come to many of our nonresistant convictions. However, when we were there, walking about the remains and seeing the mountain of shoes, the eyeglasses, and the countless piles of luggage and personal belongings of the slain Jews, we were moved. When we saw the pictures of the abuse and torture, and then walked right up to an oven actually used to burn the bodies of the Jews that were killed in the gas chambers, we rose up with indignation. When we read of Stalin's genocide, the many African massacres, and even the damage caused by the atomic bombs at Hiroshima and Nagasaki, we were moved to do something.

New Weapons

When I considered conflict in a much deeper sense than my personal loss or childhood squabbles—when I thought of these "Hitlers," "Stalins," and now even this new foe, Saddam Hussein, I realized that quietly doing nothing—was out of the question.

In his letter to the Ephesians, Paul distinctly clarified the issue: "For we wrestle not against flesh and blood." This was clear to me. What impressed me was that the verse did not stop with the mere statement "we wrestle not." It went on to say that we do indeed wrestle, not in the flesh, but "against principalities, against powers, against the rulers of the darkness of this world, against spiritual wickedness in high places" (Ephesians 6:12).

I had to ask myself if I really believed in those weapons and if I actually was willing to participate in this battle. In another place, writing to the Corinthians, Paul distinguished between the battles of the world and the battles that Christians are to participate in, saying:

> "For though we walk in the flesh, we do not war after the flesh: (For the weapons of our warfare are not carnal, but mighty through God to the pulling down of strong holds ;) Casting down imaginations, and every high thing that exalteth itself against the knowledge of God, and bringing into captivity every thought to the obedience of Christ" (2 Corinthians 10:3–7).

Those words still hit me strong today. On the one hand, Paul makes it very clear that "we do not war after the flesh," and furthermore, that our weapons are not made out of things of this earth. But again, he does not leave us there. He challenged the Corinthians that they should still be fighting, only in a different and more powerful way. It is not cowardice that God desires. He wants us to fight and do battle. Again, it is the nature of the Kingdom and the weapons of our warfare that have changed.

Real Captives

I asked myself, "Am I, through the sword of the Spirit, casting down sinful and destructive imaginations? Am I appropriating these spiritual instruments of war in my own life and implementing the shield of faith and the helmet of salvation in reality? Am I truly employing the battle tactic of having my feet shod with the Gospel of peace, and taking every thought captive?

I knew that the armies of the world clearly understood what captives were. At times throughout history, the conquering king even marched into the newly conquered city with a train of shackled prisoners behind him, showing everyone who was most powerful. Could I show the Lord a train of evil, lustful, prideful thoughts taken captive by the power of His Spirit? I pondered how these weapons Paul was talking about could be mightier than carnal instruments such as battleships and nuclear missiles.

I felt I couldn't just give up the weapons of the world and be passive. I must put on the weapons of God and arm myself with spiritual weapons such as prayer, fasting, and Gospel preaching. The early Christians understood this type of battle. Tertullian spoke on the power given to the church through prayer. He said that prayer can be used

> "To transform the weak, to restore the sick, to

purge the possessed, to open prison-bars, to loose the bonds of the innocent. Likewise [prayer] washes away faults, repels temptations, extinguishes persecutions, consoles the faint-spirited, cheers the high-spirited, escorts travelers, appeases waves, makes robbers stand aghast, nourishes the poor, governs the rich, upraises the fallen, arrests the falling, confirms the standing.

Prayer is the wall of faith: her arms and missiles against the foe who keeps watch over us on all sides. And, so never walk we unarmed. By day, be we mindful of Station; by night, of vigil. Under the arms of prayer guard we the standard of our General; await we in prayer the angel's trump."[2]

Oh, how my heart still is encouraged today when I realize the resources that God has given His church! God is still teaching me how to use these weapons more and more. It is not enough to be nonresistant. I must engage in battle with the mighty weapons that God has charged me to use.

Chapter Thirteen
The Theology of Martyrdom

"Just try to imagine that the pattern is called a 'lamb'. That alone is a scandal to the natural mind. Who has any desire to be a lamb?"

Søren Kierkegaard

But there was more...as I studied the life of Jesus and the early Christians, I realized that as powerful and necessary as things such as preaching, prayer, and fasting are in Christian warfare, there is still one more weapon that surpasses all the others. The more I studied the life of Christ and the testimony of the saints who have gone before us, the more I realized that the Christian's most ultimate weapon, his most formidable instrument of force, his most indestructible garrison against all attacks, and his most fierce arsenal against all enemies, is the cross.

The cross of Jesus Christ towers as an eternal witness to the futility of man's strength, resources, and good ideas. In his letter to the Corinthian church, warning them about the foolishness of fleshly resources, the Apostle Paul taught that the true way to win does not come by might, but by the power of laying down our life, even to the point of death. He wrote: "For the message of the cross is foolishness to those who are perishing, but to us who are being saved it is the power of God. For it is written: 'I will destroy the wisdom of the wise, And bring to nothing the understanding of the prudent'. Where is the wise? Where is the scribe? Where is the disputer of this age? Has not God made foolish the wisdom of this world?"[1]

Sheep Before Wolves

In the Gospel of Matthew, when Jesus was sending out his first group of missionaries, He gave them a graphic description of what they would experience ahead. From an earthly perspective, His depiction seemed pretty discouraging. He said, "Behold, I send you out as sheep in the midst of wolves."[2] Now, just imagine that scene in your minds for a moment. A fluffy white sheep standing there, defenseless, surrounded by a pack of growling, hungry, teeth-glaring wolves. It's not exactly an image that engenders bravery and confidence. Nevertheless, it's just the image Jesus chose to give them as an accurate picture of their ministry.

In the Sermon on the Mount, Jesus sums up his description of the "blessed" with "Blessed are ye, when men shall revile you, and persecute you, and shall say all manner of evil against you falsely, for my sake. Rejoice, and be exceeding glad: for great is your reward in heaven: for so persecuted they the prophets which were before you" (Matthew 5:11–12).

The Early Christians understood this principle. Writing in the year A.D. 190 Tertullian said:

> "The Lord will save them in that day—even His people—like sheep…No one gives the name of 'sheep' to those who fall in battle with arms in hand, or those who are killed when repelling force with force. Rather, it is given only to those who are slain, yielding themselves up in their own place of duty and with patience—rather than fighting in self-defense."[3]

Are Ye Able to Drink My Cup?

When James and John requested to be on Jesus' right and left sides in the Kingdom, Jesus turned to them, and reflecting on his approaching crucifixion, challenged them, "You do not know what you ask. Are you able to drink the cup that I am about to drink, and be baptized with the baptism that I am baptized with?"[4] They both answered back with confidence saying, "We are able." Jesus then looked right through them, into their souls and into their futures and said, "You will indeed drink My cup, and be baptized with the baptism that I am baptized with."[5]

Scripture tells us that James lost his head in Rome and that John was exiled on the deserted island of Patmos. As Jesus prophesied, they did indeed experience His baptism of the cross. As a matter fact, the life that followed all the apostles was one the world would have considered an unmitigated failure. But Christ called them "blessed." Here is just a small list of the faithful "blessed":

James—beheaded
Philip—crucified
Matthew—slain by the sword
James, son of Alpheus—stoned to death
Matthias—stoned and then beheaded
Andrew—crucified on an X-shaped cross
Peter—crucified upside-down
Paul—beheaded under the orders of Nero in Rome
Jude—crucified
Bartholomew—beaten to death with clubs
Thomas—speared to death
Simon the Zealot—crucified
John—exiled to Patmos

They might have died horrible deaths, but to God they were shining examples of faithfulness. Perhaps the biggest tool of the enemy is the fear of death. So much of our life effort is spent trying to avoid suffering and death. In contrast, Jesus told us to take up our cross daily and follow Him.[6] When the Apostle Peter suggested to Jesus that He should not go to Jerusalem because He would most likely suffer there and be killed, Jesus sharply rebuked him:

> "But He turned and said to Peter, 'Get behind Me, Satan! You are an offense to Me, for you are not mindful of the things of God, but the things of men.' Then Jesus said to His disciples, 'If anyone desires to come after Me, let him deny himself, and take up his cross, and follow Me. For whoever desires to save his life will lose it, but whoever loses his life for My sake will find it.'" [7]

Strange to our human understanding, Jesus tells us that grasping this crucified life will strengthen and actually encourage us. In the upper room, just before His crucifixion, Jesus told His apostles:

> "These things I have spoken to you, that you should not be made to stumble. They will put you out of the synagogues; yes, the time is coming that whoever kills you will think that he offers God service. And these things they will do to you because they have not known the Father nor Me. But these things I have told you, that when the time comes, you may remember that I told you of them…These things I have spoken to you, that in Me you may have peace. In the world you will have tribulation; but be of good cheer, I have overcome the world."[8]

How can I have "good cheer" in suffering and death? It seems ridiculous. However, even in my life, I can testify that time and time again, I have come to the realization that more of me had to die. Each time I went through it, it hurt. But on the other side, I always experienced more of Christ, and in a much deeper and much more intimate way.

Death Even in the Little Things

One of those defining moments took place just a few years ago. It was at a time when Brother Denny Kenaston had called several of us men to a challenging time of early morning prayer together. We were meeting three days a week, extremely early in the morning, literally hours before our work day began. Eventually, it really started to wear me out physically. As I prayed about it, I felt clear that this was from the Lord, so I began to look for physiological reasons why this must *somehow* be good for my body. I even began to research how much sleep a person really needs. I kept looking at it from several different angles, trying to convince myself that somehow all of this was actually healthy. Finally one morning, Brother Mark Brubaker said very matter-of-factly, "You know, we're all probably going to die earlier because of this."

As strange as it may sound, that statement completely liberated me! I felt free to die to myself and live to what I believed Christ had called me to. Now, don't get me wrong. I believe in being healthy, getting enough sleep, and being a good stewards of our bodies in general. It is just that at times, God calls us to things that are flat not healthy for us—martyrdom, in particular, would be one of them!

To Die Is Gain!

The Apostle Paul lived his life on the cross. His motto was: "For to me to live is Christ, and to die is gain."[9] When he discipled the churches under him, he expected them to follow his example of love, patience, and even suffering. To Timothy he wrote:

> "Now you followed my teaching, conduct, purpose, faith, patience, love, perseverance, persecutions, and sufferings, such as happened to me at Antioch, at Iconium and at Lystra; what persecutions I endured, and out of them all the Lord rescued me! Indeed, all who desire to live godly in Christ Jesus will be persecuted."[10]

The bottom line is that the early Christians had no fear of death. To die was to be with the Lord. Therefore, to compromise the teachings of Christ, even for the sake of life, was unthinkable. In the early church, the emperors bragged of their killing of the Christians. The Early Christians remarkably replied—"The blood of the martyr is seed!" The more the Christians were killed, the more they grew.

Today, when the skeptic challenges and questions Christ's followers with endless "what if's," the cross answers them all:

- What if Hitler would never have been stopped?
- What if another Hitler comes?
- What if Islam gets out of control?
- What if communism makes a come back?
- What if someone hits you first?
- What if someone shoots your grandmother?
- What if someone attacks your family?

- What if someone kicks your dog?
- What if you get killed on the mission field?
- What if a snake bites you?
- What if you lose your job?
- What if your family rejects you?

Where do these questions lead? Obviously the only goal in mind with questions such as these is the preservation of this current life and the attempted safeguard of our "happiness." Unfortunately, these questions have no end but to skirt around the cross. But once we accept the cross, suddenly the world has nothing with which to assail us! It is the Christian nuclear weapon!

The Christian Nuclear Weapon

Nowhere is this Christian nuclear weapon more emphatically articulated than in the eighth chapter of Paul's letter to the Romans. This chapter is the "Theology of Martyrdom" in a nutshell. Take a moment and conjure up any and every "what if" that you can possibly imagine. Now, with a fresh insight, re-read these words of Romans. I can remember the first time I read the chapter in this way. It was liberating! Beginning at verse 35:

> "Who shall separate us from the love of Christ? Shall tribulation, or distress, or persecution, or famine, or nakedness, or peril, or sword? As it is written: "For Your sake we are killed all day long; We are accounted as sheep for the slaughter."

Now, read that last line again—"For Your sake we are killed all day long; We are accounted as sheep for the slaughter."

Can you believe that he said that? Read it one more time, and this time actually try to envision the sheep being slaughtered:

> "As it is written: 'For Your sake we are killed all day long; We are accounted as sheep for the slaughter.'"

Okay, now, keep reading: "Yet in all these things"— What *things*? Remember, he said things such as famine, nakedness, peril, sword, and being slaughtered like a sheep!

> "Yet in all these things we are more than conquerors through Him who loved us. For I am persuaded that neither death nor life, nor angels nor principalities nor powers, nor things present nor things to come, nor height nor depth, nor any other created thing, shall be able to separate us from the love of God which is in Christ Jesus our Lord."[11]

That is the "theology of martyrdom." Did he leave anything out? The way I read it, he covered just about everything. Paul takes biblical nonresistance beyond merely refusing to participate in war to cover every aspect of our lives. The world constantly tells me that I should do everything in my life to seek health and happiness. Jesus said, "Most assuredly, I say to you, unless a grain of wheat falls into the ground and dies, it remains alone; but if it dies, it produces much grain."[12]

My flesh tells me to do everything to pamper and preserve myself. In contrast, the Apostle Paul, who understood that resurrection power exists side by side with the cross, wanted to "know Him and the power of His resurrection, and the fellowship of His sufferings, being conformed to His death."[13]

Lawsuits

Even in everyday things, my flesh lies to me and tells me that God wouldn't want me to be taken advantage of or to be considered a "door mat." At times, it is easy to have a nonresistant attitude about war, but when it comes to business and personal offenses, I can act just like the world. But Paul applies the cross to my personal life just as much as to warfare. Specifically addressing personal offenses and lawsuits Paul said, "Now therefore, it is already an utter failure for you that you go to law against one another. Why do you not rather accept wrong? Why do you not rather let yourselves be cheated?"[14]

More and more, I realize that when I die to myself, I can let more of Christ and less of me be manifested. Moreover, when I suffer for Him, I find that I am not suffering alone, but I actually am allowing the life of Christ to be lived out through me. To be dead to myself and alive to Christ is to allow Christ's suffering to be lived out in me. As Paul said to the Romans, "I beseech you therefore, brethren, by the mercies of God, that ye present your bodies a living sacrifice, holy, acceptable unto God, which is your reasonable service."[15]

Power of Forgiveness

From 1948 to 1994, South Africa maintained legalized racial discrimination. The Afrikaans' called this segregation "Apartheid." During this time, horrible acts of violence and cruelty were committed based solely on the color of someone's skin. After 1994, once apartheid was over, a new government was set up under Nelson Mandela. Soon after he was in leadership, Mandela set up an investigative commission called "Truth and Reconciliation Commission" that looked into many of these acts of racial violence and human rights violations. Many former government and military officials were brought to trial and punished. John D. Roth, in his book, *Choosing Against War* says that

> "At one meeting early in their work, the commission gathered to reach a verdict on a particularly painful case involving an elderly South African woman. At the hearing, a group of white police officers, led by a Mr. Van de Broek admitted their personal responsibility in the death of her 18-year-old son. They acknowledged shooting the young man at point blank range, setting his body on fire, and then partying around the fire until the body had been reduced to little more than ashes.
>
> Eight years later, Van de Broek and his fellow officers had again intersected with the woman's life, this time to take her husband into captivity. And then, some time later, Van de Broek had come knocking at her door once more. Rousing her from bed in the dead of night, he brought the woman to an isolated set-

ting by a river where her husband lay tied to a pile of wood. As she watched, he and the officers doused the man with gasoline and then ignited a fire. The last words her husband spoke to her, in the midst of the blazing pyre, were, 'Forgive them.'

Now at long last the time had come for justice to be served. Those involved had confessed their guilt, and the Commission turned to the woman for a final statement regarding her desire for an appropriate punishment.

'I want three things,' the woman said calmly. 'I want Mr. Van de Broek to take me to the place where they burned my husband's body. I would like to gather up the dust and give him a decent burial.'

'Second, Mr. Van de Broek took all my family away from me, so I still have a lot of love to give. Twice a month, I would like for him to come to the ghetto and spend a day with me so I can be a mother to him.'

'Third, I would like Mr. Van de Broek to know that he is forgiven by God, and that I forgive him, too. And, I would like someone to come and lead me by the hand to where Mr. Van de Broek is so that I can embrace him and he can know my forgiveness is real.'

As the elderly woman made her way across the silent courtroom, Van de Broek reportedly fainted, overcome by emotion. And then the silence was broken when someone began singing, 'Amazing Grace.' Others soon picked up the words of the familiar hymn, so that finally the entire audience in the courtroom was joined in song."[16]

What a testimony of love! Everything that had been dear to this woman was brutally taken from her. Yet somehow, she was able to die to her losses, her pain, her regrets and her rights and was able to reach out and hug the very man that caused all her pain—*How?*

...Because there was something more real in this elderly woman's life than life itself—more true than temporal circumstances—and more meaningful than any earthly reward. She had died to herself years before and was *alive* in Christ—nothing could take that away from her!

Gelassenheit

In 1527, shortly after the beginning of the Radical Reformation, laws were quickly passed against the Anabaptists, by both the Catholics and the Protestants. Some sixty of these radical, early Anabaptist reformers met in Augsburg, Switzerland, to discuss mission, theology, and church planting. Historians later called this little meeting "The Martyrs' Synod" because within a few years of this meeting, nearly all the men present were martyred.

Immediately after the meeting, laws were being passed everywhere to put these new radicals to death. The cruelest of these laws was a decision of the Swabian League passed at Augsburg authorizing a band of four hundred armed horsemen to hunt the Anabaptists down and bring them to headquarters. All who would not recant were burned at the stake without trial. Those who did recant were beheaded. Women were executed by drowning. One eyewitness during this time was quoted saying, "It is such a misery, that the whole city of Augsburg is saddened. They are daily beheading some, at times four or six, and at times ten persons."[17]

One of the men present at that Martyrs' Synod, anticipating their nearly certain martyrdom, described their plight with almost unnatural resolve, saying that their lives were ready to be offered to God, like food being given to the farmer. He said that with animals, the lower creatures exist for the sake of higher ones. He said many plants and animals fulfill their destiny through being killed and consumed by humans. Similarly, humans attain their destiny through crucifixion. He said that these experiences purge and prepare them for communion with God, especially as they share in the crucifixion of His Son.[18]

These were fitting words for all those present because five years later, only two of the original sixty men were still alive. Today, the German term that has come down through the years to describe this kind of total humility and yieldedness to the will of God is the word "Gelassenheit." It is the "theology of martyrdom." I believe that without Gelassenheit, biblical nonresistance is nonsense.

Martyrdom of Loved Ones

When the joy of the cross is fully embraced, we can accept God's will, even for our loved ones. As discussed in the previous chapter, the best thing that we could ever do for our families is to entrust them to Jesus Christ.

One such case of trusting God, even when it might mean the death of a loved one, comes from the story about the wife of John Welsh. When the king of England banished John to France, he quickly learned French and began preaching to the persecuted church there. Later, when his health started to decline, his wife pleaded with King James to let him return to England because he was dying from the conditions in France. King James said he could return if he would submit to the English bishops. After being challenged with this compromise, John Welsh's wife simply lifted up her apron and replied, "I would rather have his head cut off and placed in my apron then have him betray the Truth!"[19] She loved her husband, but she loved the rewards of Christ for her husband even more. She knew it would be more important for him to be faithful to the end!

The Theology of Martyrdom in Heaven

In the book of Revelation, chapter five, the Apostle John describes a scene of heaven that is so far beyond the values, attitudes, logic, and goals of this present world that only an inspired text could begin to do it justice. He describes a scene in which God, high and lifted up, is seated upon His throne with a giant book in his hand, sealed tightly with seven very strong seals. Wanting to reveal the contents of the book, a strong angel cried out:

"Who is worthy to open the scroll and to loose its seals?"[20]

As that question rang out through Heaven, it was discovered that no man, either in heaven or on earth, was found worthy to open it!

Moved by the scene, John tells us that he began to cry, and that he cried a lot. But as he was there crying, an angel came up to him and told him to stop crying because they finally had found someone strong and worthy enough to open the seals. This person was described to John as a lion:

"The Lion of the tribe of Judah, the Root of David, has prevailed to open the scroll and to loose its seven seals."[21]

I wondered, "What must John have been thinking at that time?" He might have wondered who would be powerful and holy enough to open such seals. He might have thought, "Of course, a lion of the root of David, that sounds powerful enough!"

But then, as John looked up with the anticipation of seeing this strong and mighty lion, he was directed right to the center of the throne of God, where his eyes beheld instead—a slaughtered lamb.

> "And I looked, and behold, in the midst of the throne and of the four living creatures, and in the midst of the elders, stood a Lamb as though it had been slain, having seven horns and seven eyes, which are the seven Spirits of God sent out into all the earth. Then He came and took the scroll out of the right hand of Him who sat on the throne."[22]

After that, John saw that this slain lamb boldly took the book and opened it. Next, he describes a scene in which millions of people, gathered from every country on earth, are praising and worshiping this slain lamb, singing to him a "new song":

"And they sang a new song, saying: 'You are worthy to take the scroll, And to open its seals; For You were slain, And have redeemed us to God by Your blood Out of every tribe and tongue and people and nation, And have made us kings and priests to our God; And we shall reign on the earth.'"[23]

I thought, "I want to worship this slain lamb and be in His Kingdom!" I long to sing that "new song" with them!

Chapter Fourteen
Him or It?

Day of the court hearing

The most intimidating hurdle of the entire conscientious objection request process was the final court hearing. It was the culmination of all the interviews, written papers, chaplain visits, psychologist interviews, and everything in-between. In some ways, we dreaded this hearing because we knew that we could be accepted or rejected depending solely on how we fared in this interview. Each of us had to go individually and stand trial alone.

A few days before the hearing, the Mennonite Central Committee sent us a little booklet in the mail on how to answer some of the more common questions typically thrown out during these hearings. When I realized what it was, I started to open it and look at some of the answers. But suddenly, after I started to look at it, I had an overwhelming feeling to put the book away. Then I remembered a powerful promise that Jesus gave for moments just like these: "Now when they bring you to the synagogues and magistrates and authorities, do not worry about how or what you should answer, or what you should say. For the Holy Spirit will teach you in that very hour what you ought to say."[1] I took that promise, closed the book, and trusted in the Holy Spirit to give me all the answers I would need.

The Court Room

A few days later, standing before the "magistrates and authorities," I actually got to put this promise into practice. The court room was set up fairly informally. A long table stood at the front with another small table coming off of it at the end, so that it resembled the shape of a capital "T". The "judge" was a young

African American captain from the Justice Department. He sat at the front of the table with a stack of papers, a laptop computer, and several books. One of the main focal points before him was my application for conscientious objector status. Sitting directly across the table from me was Andre' Stoner, a counselor sent out from the Mennonite Central Committee to Germany to help soldiers with the conscientious objector process. It was such a comfort to have him there.

It all started with the customary attention and salute, and then the judge asked me to take a seat. Then he began asking me every conceivable question related to war and nonresistance. He asked me about my conversion, and how I felt about other wars. He asked me what I thought about Hitler, Saddam Hussein, and the Communists. He asked me how I felt about specific police actions that America was involved with in Central America. He asked me if I owned a gun, and he even asked me how I felt about hunting. With each question, I whispered a little prayer and trusted the Holy Spirit to give me the answer. I tried not to just give him "canned" answers, but rather, to minister a portion of Scripture when I could.

I remember he asked me one question about the harassment that I was receiving from my fellow soldiers in my company. He wanted to know if I "enjoyed" this harassment. I suppose he was questioning whether I was just looking for trouble. In answer to this, I told him that I did not enjoy the harassment in the flesh, but that I did consider it a privilege. I opened my Bible to Matt 5:10–11, and read:

> "Blessed are those who have been persecuted for the sake of righteousness, for theirs is the

kingdom of heaven. Blessed are you when people insult you and persecute you, and falsely say all kinds of evil against you because of Me. Rejoice and be glad, for your reward in heaven is great; for in the same way they persecuted the prophets who were before you."

Then I said, "I guess that's how I feel." He was respectful, almost kind, and I could tell that he had some knowledge of the Bible. At some points, I felt that his questions were almost searching.

Tania and the other couple who went through all of this with us, Rick and Dawn Shirley, had experiences just as grueling as mine. When it was all over, we were so relieved. We didn't know it at the time, but it would be eight long months from the time we submitted our application until we received the results of our request.

Time to Study

Initially, after we had started the whole process, the Army still had us playing our instruments and singing in the concert band. That all ended one day when I told the commander that I felt somewhat hypocritical to be singing the song "God bless the USA" because there was a line in it that said, "I would gladly stand up next to her and defend her still today." He didn't like that very much.

For the rest of our time in the Army, until we heard from the Pentagon about our results, we were shuffled around to a strange variety of odd jobs. We did anything from being music librarians, to painting latrines, to painting ancient rusty old handrails that literally were disintegrating with every stroke of the paintbrush. I suppose the most interesting assignment was that of working as journalists for the base newspaper.

Those eight months gave us lots of time to grow in God and explore His will for our lives. We read lots of books, prayed, studied our Bibles, and eventually met with various groups of unconventional, committed, and sometimes peculiar Christians. Our attention to nonresistance naturally attracted us to many new people and groups who held similar convictions. This was a blessing in many ways, but it also was a great challenge and, at times, a big disappointment. I found myself coming into a world of people who were saying many of the same things I was, but often meaning something completely different.

Buddhist Baptists and U2 Groupies

One such instance was the time Tania and I held a little get-together in our apartment at Hochspeyer, Germany, for all those soldiers who currently were getting out of the Army as conscientious objectors. This was an eye-opener for me. I guess I had the mistaken impression that anyone becoming a conscientious objector would naturally be some kind of a sold-out, radical Christian. But I was wrong.

During the meeting, I had a time for people to share their "testimonies." One guy said he became a conscientious objector because of the lyrics of a U2 song. Another man said it was because he was trying to be both a Baptist and a Buddhist! (I still haven't figured that one out!) Several others were doing so for merely humanitarian reasons. There were a few civilians there as well. We could all talk about war and peace, but honestly, it didn't seem that most wanted to talk about Jesus.

Soon after, Tania and I were invited to a nuclear bomb protest outside some military base. Against my better judgment, we went, and there we stood with a host of "peace people" shouting "No more nukes! No more nukes!" I was trying to find myself, or at least I was trying to find "my people," and I was having a very hard time. Somehow this just didn't seem like the saints I read about in the *Martyrs Mirror*, or the martyrs of the early church. It seemed that many of these people had a cause, but you had to wonder if they had Christ.

This was a hard time for me. Admittedly, we were very idealistic. We had read about the saints and martyrs throughout history, and we were earnest about finding them living now in our current day. We visited a little community of people all residing in one big apartment building. They were determined to live in community, and that impressed us. But when we visited, it just seemed like something was missing.

Trip to an "Anabaptist" College

Jumping ahead a bit—one of the hardest visits came when we actually were out of the Army. We had the opportunity to visit a college that claimed to be based on Anabaptist theology and principles. To us, the very idea of an Anabaptist college seemed like a utopia! "Just imagine," I thought to myself, "a whole college of young Anabaptist men and women all striving for a radical relationship with Jesus Christ!"

We had been invited to consider enrollment for the next semester, so we flew out to this college with high expectations, ready to give our testimony and learn more about this school. It was right at the very beginning of the school year, so classes were just getting started. We were so excited! We could hardly wait to meet these people who we had formerly only read about!

I'm Not a Peace Activist

Now…I must admit that we were very idealistic. We got off that plane with such a romanticized view of the Anabaptists that we practically had the *Martyrs Mirror* under one arm and the *Complete Writings of Menno Simons* under the other! We needed a "reality check." We still had a lot of hard lessons to learn.

All that said, we were pretty surprised by what we found. Our first stop was the "Peace Club." I thought that this would be perfect. It was their first meeting of the semester, so they were making all kinds of plans for the upcoming year. At the beginning, we just sat on one side of the table while the young men discussed their plans for the year with one another.

But as I listened, my heart sank. As they discussed their ideas, some of the activities they mentioned were startling. The talk was very political: protest, sarcasm, and general anti-government issues took center stage.

A discussion about homosexuality came up, and surprisingly, the Peace Club discussed plans for a closer relationship and greater support for the gay and lesbian society at the secular college across town. As they discussed the homosexuality issue, they didn't talk about the need for helping these people come to repentance. Instead, they excused their sin and said that these people should be looked on as a "persecuted minority group."

Near the end of their discussion someone suggested a "pro-life" versus "pro-choice" debate on campus. They all thought that was a good idea until another young man reminded them that the guy who was the pro-life advocate had graduated last year!

After all these discussions, the leader looked at me and asked if I had any questions for them. I paused and thought for a moment. Then I said, "I have only one question. But I would like to go down the line and have each of you answer it individually."

"Okay," they replied, "ask anything you wish."

"This is a peace club, right?"

"Right."

"Could each of you simply tell me why you believe in 'peace?'"

One by one, the answers came. Some had to do with the oppression of the poor. Some believed in peace because of the damage caused by wars. For some, it was for the sake of the environment or the hungry. Finally, right at the end, a very young-looking, red-headed freshman said, "It's because of the words of Jesus."

I stopped them and said, "That's it! That's what I wanted to hear." I went on to say that I was not a peace activist. "I'm just a Christian." I explained. "Nonresistance is a *part* of Christianity, but it's not the whole. There are a lot of other wonderful teachings in the Bible besides nonresistance." I reassured them that we obviously felt very strongly about the importance of nonresistance. However, our focus, our attention, and our driving passion was Christ.

Tania and I repeated this testimony to several classes and groups. Some were very excited, but some looked a bit concerned. The short of it was that we left there with a sinking "reality check" and a question mark about our future.

Off Center

In keeping with their Anabaptist traditions, pacifism was an important doctrine to the students at this college. However, it seemed that somewhere the doctrine of nonresistance had moved far away from its source. No longer were the words of Scripture the focus and driving passion behind the doctrine. Pacifism had nearly become an end to itself.

Later, when I challenged one of them for defending homosexuality, he argued that homosexuals are created this way from birth, so we should just accept them and ignore the sin.

I argued that I too had been born with many sinful desires. For instance, the natural desire to defend myself and hate my enemies was built deep within me. However, after being confronted with the words of Scripture, I had to repent of this behavior. If I had allowed myself to justify my sinful behavior by calling it a "built-in desire of my people group," then I would still be in the Army.

Disclaimer

I should mention that we also met many committed Christians at this college. Some of the older people with whom we stayed and many of the staff that we had the privilege to meet lived a remarkably simple lifestyle and expressed a genuine hospitality in a way that really challenged us.

It was just that in the end we saw that these young people were dangerously close to letting the issues of peace and nonresistance become their entire focus. As a result they were not centering on the person of Jesus Christ. Because of this, they were easily dismissing other parts of Christ's teachings. Tania and I were passionate believers in biblical nonresistance, but ultimately, we knew we wanted *"Him"* not "it."

Searching for Kingdom Christians

As I read and talked, both to Christians who supported nonresistance and those who rejected it, I began to notice that there were two diametrically opposing opinions concerning the Christian's place in warfare. These opinions tended to polarize to the farthest right and the farthest left.

The far right view obviously rejects the teaching of nonresistance, but more than this, they actually champion the place of Christians at all levels of government. They see politics and commerce as an indispensable way to propagate the Kingdom of God. Again, I would hear them refer to the passage in Romans 13 as a defense that the Emperor (in our case the President) "does not bear the sword in vain; for he is God's minister, an avenger to execute wrath on him who practices evil."[2]

On the other hand, to the far left, shocked and dismayed at the theocratic vocabulary of the far right, were people who virtually had thrown out everything distinctly Christian except "love your enemies." What I found surprising about this "leftist" group was just how theocratically political they had become as well. The idea of not entangling ourselves in the affairs of this world seemed to be violated just as much by the liberal-pacifist camp as it was by the Christian-militant camp. Christians everywhere are universally called to be sojourners, pilgrims, and strangers on this earth, ruled and governed by Christ, alone—not some new, global social order.

On the one hand, the idea of a peace activist rising to power, legislating nonresistance, self-denial, and pacifism is intellectually embarrassing in a depraved, non-redeemed world. Moreover, the protesting, picketing, lobbying, and bullying of political opponents by leftist activists hardly seems to personify Christ. On the other hand, to rule by force, politics, and economics, even tacitly in the name of Christ, is nothing short of blasphemy. I felt that both of these extremes were too close to Paul's warnings about worldly fraternization.

A Growing Remnant

During that eight-month wait for the results of our conscientious objector applications, we did find some likeminded fellowship. Once, while my wife and I were praying in a chow hall before our meal, a young Christian man noticed and came up to talk with us. He invited us to his little fellowship. We were very blessed there, and through these believers, we were stretched and challenged about many areas of our lives.

As we have continued in our journey, we have discovered that, spread all over the earth, there literally are thousands of believers turning to the teachings of

Christ, and being fools enough to believe every word of His teachings. Amazingly, it seems that many times, when someone notices that another person actually is taking the words of Jesus literally and trying to live them out, the attraction is nearly irresistible. I love to listen to their testimonies, to see the spark in their eyes, and to hear the words of Jesus on their lips. When I hear these testimonies, I know that, just like my wife and me, they too will never be the same. Not surprisingly, these new believers also love to tell others about their decision to follow Jesus radically, and this trend is growing.

The Spreading Seed

In one of the most impressive parables of Jesus, He likened the Kingdom of God to a mustard seed:

> "Another parable He put forth to them, saying: 'The kingdom of heaven is like a mustard seed, which a man took and sowed in his field, which indeed is the least of all the seeds; but when it is grown it is greater than the herbs and becomes a tree, so that the birds of the air come and nest in its branches.'"[3]

What does a mustard tree look like? Shane Claiborne has recently said about the mustard tree:

> "Plenty of people had lofty expectations of the kingdom coming in spectacular triumph and were familiar with the well-known "cedars of Lebanon" imagery from the prophets, who described the kingdom as the greatest of all trees, not unlike a giant redwood tree...But Jesus

ridiculed this triumphal expectation. After all, even mature mustard plants stand only a few feet high, modest little bushes. The Jesus revolution is not a frontal attack on the empires of the world. It is a subtle contagion, spreading one little life, one little hospitality house, at a time."[4]

Is the "theology of martyrdom" practical? To the flesh, it is foolishness, but when I embrace it in all parts of my life by faith, it is absolutely liberating.

The Truth in the Last Days

Regardless of the timing of your eschatology, in the book of Revelation a day is predicted when the world is in absolute chaos with the Antichrist roaring and warfare raging. John describes three distinguishing marks that identify the people of God. In these distinguishing marks, John describes how the Christians will stand out and persevere.

Describing the times, in Revelation 13, John tells us that the Antichrist actually will be given power to defeat the saints:

"It was granted to him to make war with the saints and to overcome them. And authority was given him over every tribe, tongue, and nation. All who dwell on the earth will worship him, whose names have not been written in the Book of Life of the Lamb slain from the foundation of the world."[5]

Why would God give the antichrist power to kill the saints? This question is right up there with the question "Why did God give Pilate the power to kill Jesus?"

Somehow, the saints' defiance of death and uncompromising loyalty to God is an ultimate blow to Satan, and the ultimate praise to our God. But then he makes the solemn proclamation: "If any man have an ear, let him hear"—that means we better listen! He then offers the first identifying mark of the saints in the last days:

> "He who leads into captivity shall go into captivity; he who kills with the sword must be killed with the sword. Here is the patience and the faith of the saints."[6]

Incredibly, the very principle taught by Jesus when He told Peter to put away his sword actually becomes one of the defining marks of the saints in the last days. In the next chapter, John gives the other two identifying marks of the saints in the last days:

> "Here is the patience of the saints; here are those who keep the commandments of God and the faith of Jesus."[7]

Therefore, when times get to their absolute worst, we are going to recognize the saints of God by those who are:

- A holy people who keep the teachings of Jesus.
- A people who have a genuine faith in Christ.
- A people who practice the principle established by Christ to Peter, when He said, "Put your sword in its place, for all who take the sword will perish by the sword."[8]

The culmination of this "last days" theology is all capped off by John's surprising revelation that in the end, this defenseless, dying army actually wins! But what's most surprising is that the antichrist is stopped—

not by guns, bombs, or resourceful politics—but by the blood and faith of the martyrs.

John says, "And they overcame him by the blood of the Lamb, and by the word of their testimony; and they loved not their lives unto the death."[9] That's *Gelassenheit*—that's the "theology of martyrdom"—that's the cross—that's real victory!

The Results and the Surprise

At last, after approximately eight long months of waiting, we finally were notified that the same captain who had conducted our hearing wanted to meet with us upstairs in our first sergeant's office to give us the results of our conscientious objector applications. This was what we had waited for! I tried to act confident, but inside I was scared. The first sergeant challenged me, "What are you gonna' do if he says no?"

Shocked by his challenge, I simply replied, "I don't know; we would certainly have to pray about it." Once the captain arrived, we were summoned to report to the designated office. Here we were, once again making our way up those creaky stairs.

My mind went back to all that had happened over the past year. A lot had transpired since our little band of pilgrims had first marched up these stairs together and laid our applications on the commander's desk to initiate this whole process. Together we had prayed, read, and learned so much since that day. It had been quite a journey.

As we neared the room, my mind replayed the stories of court marshals and jail time that the military newspaper was playing up recently. Reaching the door,

I knocked, whispered a million prayers, and once again entered the room.

This time, we were in the first sergeant's office. It was tiny. I don't think it could have been much more than about eight by ten feet. Facing us was a military desk. All four of us crowded in, came to attention, and saluted the captain. The captain returned the salute and called us to be "at ease." Right on the edge of the desk, among several other randomly scattered papers, sat four thick manila envelopes. The captain pointed to them and said,

"These are the results of your conscientious objector applications. We will review them in a minute. But first, I would like to offer you something."

Not knowing what to think, I just said, "Yes sir."

"I want to offer you the chance to go back and forget about all this. The war is over now. You all have nice careers. Yes, it will be embarrassing for awhile, but in time, all of that will pass. I have the authority to do this for you."

Hardly thinking I looked at Tania's eyes and the Shirleys, then quickly replied, "No sir, we are confident that God wants us to do this, so we feel we must continue."

The others confirmed this to the commander as well. I couldn't help but wonder why he was offering us this before he gave us the results.

He continued, "I thought that was what you would say. Well, alright then, I will give you the results."
We all were about to explode with anxiety!

"You all have been approved for a conscientious objector discharge."

As soon as he said it, we all rejoiced as much as we

could in a military setting. It felt as though an entire mountain had been removed and we were allowed to walk right on through! It was wonderful!

But then something marvelous happened that still to this day fills us with wonder and amazement. As we stood there rejoicing—in a military way, of course—the captain smiled and said, "But wait, before you go, there's something I need to tell you."

"Yes sir?" we nodded. "What is it?"

"I too now am getting out of the Army for the very same reasons."

"What?!"

We couldn't believe it. The very same officer who was the judge at our conscientious objector hearings was now leaving the Army "for the very same reasons"! I began to try talking to him about it and asking some questions, but it was clear that he did not feel free to talk. He quickly picked up a bunch of paper work and bade us a final "farewell."

I still can hardly believe it. The whole thing testified to me of the nearly irresistible power of Christ. This man had sat as a judge and heard four testimonies, one after another, testifying of Christ and what He had done in our lives. He had drilled us with questions and challenged us with alternative ideas. Apparently, the testimonies had left behind seeds in a fertile ground. Now, months later, those seeds were growing and this judge was surrendering to Christ and asking to get out of the Army for the same reason he had heard us give. It put a wonderful cap on all that we had been through and provided a great encouragement for what was ahead.

Chapter Fifteen
Altar Call

Rick and I hammering on the Berlin Wall

That's my story. But really it's not mine. It is just one page in the long story about Jesus and those who, like me, my wife, the Shirleys, the captain, and millions more, have heard His message, believed it, and found the grace from God to follow Him regardless of the cost. He came not as a philosopher or a politician. When Jesus came, He came as King. Remember, Jesus said to Pilate that it was for the very purpose of being a king that He was born! But remember also that He said to Pilate, "I have come into the world, that I should bear witness to the truth. Everyone who is of the truth hears My voice."[1]

"Hears His voice"…What does that mean for you and me today? It could mean a lot of things, but at the very least, it means hearing the words Jesus spoke when He was here on earth. Let me ask you, do you "hear His voice"? Many have, and their lives have never been the same.

As soon as Jesus began to preach, a revolution was started. Not a revolution of tyranny, totalitarianism, or violence, but one of self-sacrifice, compassion, and self-denial, and for many—martyrdom. While it is not a revolution of violence, it is nonetheless a revolution.

Jesus said "And from the days of John the Baptist until now the kingdom of heaven suffers violence, and the violent take it by force."[2] Or as Luke put it, "The law and the prophets were until John. Since that time the kingdom of God has been preached, and everyone is pressing into it."[3] What a glorious revolution this is. Are you one of those "pressing into it" that Jesus described?

The "violent" as Matthew put it, are the ones who are granted entrance into this kingdom. Are you one of those? Not the indifferent, not the lukewarm, not those who choose the world over the ways of Christ, but those who "press into it," as Luke pictures it.

According to the Gospel of Mark, when Jesus began his ministry by preaching the Kingdom, He offered His message to be either received or rejected: "Now after John was put in prison, Jesus came to Galilee, preaching the gospel of the kingdom of God, and saying, 'The time is fulfilled, and the kingdom of God is at hand. Repent, and believe in the gospel.'"[4]

Do you believe? Are you a follower of Christ? Do you listen to His voice? If you say yes, then you should be walking as He walked. Jesus said, "If ye love me, keep my commandments" (John 14:15).

Do You Blame the Church?

Admittedly, a lot of bad things have been done in the name of Christ through the centuries. As a matter of fact, if you were to take the Sermon on the Mount found in Matthew, chapters 5, 6, and 7 and build a church the complete opposite of everything Jesus taught, you would end up with a church that painfully resembles modern-day Christianity. At the end of the sermon, Jesus prophesied very pointedly what would happen to those who chose not to build on His teachings:

> "Everyone who hears these sayings of Mine, and does not do them, will be like a foolish man who built his house on the sand: and the rain descended, the floods came, and the winds blew and beat on that house; and it fell. And great was its fall" (Matthew 7:26–27).

So what about you and me? We could blame all the current problems on the failures of the past. We could curse the atrocities of tyrants or deride the pomp of hypocrites, but none of those things will get us closer to God. If we are honest, we will admit that oftentimes such blame is just a smoke screen to get the attention off our own sins and on to something else. Most of those who have done wrong in the past are gone now. Of such, the Bible says, "Indeed, let God be true but every man a liar."[5] Ultimately, the responsibility has now come down to you and me.

Receive a Hundredfold

Since those days when Tania and I left the Army, not having any idea where we would end up, God has led us to places we never even dreamed of! The Apostle Peter said to Jesus, "Lo, we have left all, and have fol-lowed thee."[6] What a declaration! If only Peter could have known what was in store for him. Jesus responded to his proclamation with:

> "Assuredly, I say to you, there is no one who has left house or brothers or sisters or father or mother or wife or children or lands, for My sake and the gospel's, who shall not receive a hun-dredfold now in this time—houses and brothers and sisters and mothers and children and lands, with persecutions—and in the age to come, eternal life."[7]

Ever since Jesus said that, countless souls have trusted this promise and testified that it is true. I am just one of them. I certainly can testify with Peter that the hundredfold blessing of meeting awakened souls with a light in their eyes and a love for God in their hearts has made the journey rewarding. Granted, such a walk often comes with trials and persecutions, but I have found that allegiance to His eternal Kingdom is worth it all.

Napoleon Bonaparte

At the end of his life, the defeated conqueror, Napoleon Bonaparte, began to understand the invincible Kingdom of Jesus Christ. After his defeat at Waterloo, Napoleon was taken captive by British soldiers and eventually exiled to a remote island off the coast of Africa. There, humbled by defeat and imprisonment, Napoleon realized that his kingdom had come to naught, whereas Christ's Kingdom was still marching on. Before his death, Napoleon wrote the following,

> "I know men, and I tell you that Jesus Christ is no mere man. Between him and every other person in the world there is no possible term of comparison. Alexander, Caesar, Charlemagne, and I founded empires, But on what did we rest the creations of our genius? Upon force. Jesus Christ founded His Empire upon love, and at this hour millions of people would die for Him."

Are you one of them?

The word "allegiance" carries with it quite a significant challenge. It has an Anglo-French origin and literally means "the loyalty of a subject or servant to his lord." To whom do you give your allegiance? Jesus is not asking us to despise our countries, to rebel against the establishment, or to disrespect our authorities.

But…

If our hearts are entangled in the politics and values of this world
If our weapons are carnal and not spiritual
If we make war after the flesh
If with these weapons, we destroy men's lives instead of saving them
If we are living by the sword
If we hate our enemies
If we still insist on an "eye for an eye and a tooth for a tooth,"
Then what Jesus is asking for is—*a change of allegiance.*

What about you?

Reference Guide for Conscientious Objector Applications

Overview

Often when I preach on nonresistance, one of the most common questions I hear from the young men is what to do about signing up with the Selective Service. The most common scenario seems to be that they are turning 18 and the Selective Service is knocking on their door. What should they do?

Other times, I am contacted by people still in the military who are asking what they can do if they no longer feel they can conscientiously stay in the military.

For that reason, I decided to add this little appendix. I hope it will answer a few of the more common questions. Fortunately, today quite a lot of information is available for those who find themselves in these situations. By way of a disclaimer, however, I must warn you that when you start looking for information about conscientious objection and nonresistance, you unfortunately might not always end up finding literature with God-honoring attitudes. Many times, the overall spirit is more anti-American or anti-authority and does not represent a true Christian spirit of nonresistance.

You can go to almost any library these days, especially if you are in the military, and have someone help you look up any resource you need and print it out, right there on the spot. Again, just be careful with the spirit behind many of these sites.

Witness

Most importantly, as you begin to walk through some of these things, remember, people are watching. Whether you are a Marine in Afghanistan filling out you application for conscientious objector (CO) discharge or a young Amishman from Lancaster County filling out a declaration of your beliefs, you can use this procedure as a time to strengthen your faith and witness to others. I would have never guessed that my captain, the very man who conducted the CO hearings, would later have become a CO himself.

Fill out your forms, face your interviews, and state your claim with conviction. People are listening. This process in my life proved to be one of the most spiritually uplifting times I've ever experienced.

Your Lifestyle Matters

The most significant thing you can do, whether you're in the military or coming before a draft board, is to live out your beliefs radically with conviction. What the draft board is looking for is sincerity.

Taken straight from the very regulation that guides soldiers applying for conscientious objection, AR 600-43 states

> "The most important considera-
> tion is not whether applicants
> are sincere in wanting to be
> designated as a conscientious
> objector, but whether their as-

serted convictions are sincerely held. Sincerity is determined by an impartial evaluation of each person's thinking and living in totality, past and present. The conduct of persons, in particular their outward manifestation of the beliefs asserted, will be carefully examined and given substantial weight in evaluating their application...The task is to decide whether the beliefs professed are sincerely held and whether they govern the claimant's actions in <u>word and deed</u>."

In an age when every click of your mouse and every swipe of your debit card is recorded and easily accessed, this judgment of "word and deed" could prove interesting. The truth speaks for itself. It would be embarrassing, to say the least, if you make claims that you are too scrupulous to enter the military because of your Christian convictions while your draft board has in their hand the list of the pornographic Web sites you just visited last month—not to mention the receipts they acquire of your violent military computer game purchases!

Scripture says, "For the time is come that judgment must begin at the house of God: and if it first begin at us, what shall the end be of them that obey not the gospel of God?"[1] Historically, in times of national tragedy or persecution, this has worked to purify the church.

Part 1: Registering With the Selective Service

The Central Committee for Conscientious Objectors (CCCO) says:

> "If you're male and a U.S. citizen, you're legally required to register with the Selective Service System (SSS), within thirty days before or twenty-nine days after your 18th birthday. (If you're female you don't have to register: in fact, you can't. Not that the military doesn't want you—recruiters have a special sales pitch just for women!) Most male U.S. residents who aren't citizens are also required to register.
>
> The registration form is available at your local post office. You'll be asked for your name, gender, social security number, date of birth, temporary and permanent addresses, phone numbers, and signature. The form has no space for claiming any deferments or exemptions, such as conscientious objection. Such claims could only be made after an actual draft was restarted, and you've received a draft notice."

In other words, you can't officially "register" as a CO until you actually receive draft papers telling you to report to the draft board. However, there are things you can do now that will help you to register successfully as a CO when the draft comes.

The Timing of Your Convictions

Perhaps the biggest thing the Selective Service or the CO board considers is the *timing* of your conviction. If you are a young man who has never been in the military and you are facing a possible draft, then it would be in your best interest to prove that you were a CO *before* you got your draft papers. The military is trying to distinguish between the conscientious and the cowards.

Anything that you can do to document your convictions now will prove invaluable to you before a draft board. Previous well-documented proof of your conviction before the moment of crises is your best resource when you stand before the board. The timing of this document is critical.

Filling Out Your Selective Service Card

The Center on Conscience and War gives COs some good direction about how to register with the Selective Service. They say that at a minimum, you should print in legible black ink across the middle of the registration form "I AM A CONSCIENTIOUS OBJECTOR TO WAR IN ANY FORM."

You should then make a copy of this card and keep it for your records because the Selective Service actually just logs the information into a computer and then throws it away. They also suggest that you keep a copy of this card on file with your local church, together with any other statements you have made.

Declaration of Conscientious Objection to War

In the back of this book I have included a postcard taken directly from the form that the Selective Service sends you at the time of a draft (SSS Form 22). Simply fill out this card and mail it to yourself. It will act as dated proof that you held a previous conviction against fighting. Getting it notarized would be icing on the cake, but at the very least, a stamp and dated post card would be a choice thing to have when you face your draft board meeting.

What If I Go to a "Peace Church"?

Recent military regulations state that merely belonging to a historic peace church is not enough to warrant a CO discharge. They want to see proof that you hold these convictions personally. Army regulation 600-43 states:

> "Mere affiliation with a church or other group that advocates conscientious objection as a tenet of its creed does not nec-essarily determine a person's position or belief."

This is not to say that belonging to a "peace church" would not help. In reality, it probably would do a lot to help substantiate your case. However, if the only thing you can say for yourself when you go to the draft office is "the church says so," then you could be in big trouble.

One more thing you should know is that the military recognizes only complete conscientious objection to *all* wars. They do not grant CO status to those who consider only a certain war unjust or wrong.

Part 2: If You Are Currently in the Military

If you are currently in the military and want out, then you need to prove that you have undergone a *change* in your conviction. Otherwise, they will have to assume that you originally enlisted fraudulently. The Marine Corps puts it this way:

> "A Marine who possesses qualifying beliefs which became fixed or crystallized <u>before</u> entering military service is not eligible for conscientious objector status."[2]

That underlined "<u>before</u>" in the preceding quote is from the actual regulation. I think that this underlined word demonstrates the trust of their investigation. What changed in your life? Were you born again? Did you discover the writings of the early church? Did you read the Sermon on the Mount for the first time? What was it that caused a change in your convictions since the time that you enlisted?

The Journey

The first thing you need to do is go to the library and get a copy of the regulation that governs your conscientious objection process. The regulations for the various services are listed as follows:

- Army Regulation 600-43.
- Naval Military Personnel Manual (MILPERSMAN) 1900-020, Convenience of

the Government Separation Based on Conscientious Objection.

- Marine Corps Regulation: MCO 1306.16 E.
- Air Force Regulation: AFI 36-3204.
- Coast Guard Regulation: COMDTINST 1900.8.

These documents actually are a great blessing. If you truly have had a change in your convictions since your enlistment, then these regulations can almost work in your favor. Following these procedures can help you avoid pitfalls that could lead to a dishonorable discharge. I personally can attest to the help they were to us when we went through the process.

I feel I need to mention a couple of things here. First, just like civilians filing with the Selective Service, the military recognizes only complete conscientious objection to *all* wars. They do not grant CO status to those who consider only a certain war unjust or wrong.

Second, early on they may offer you a "non-combatant" status. You need to know that if you accept this option, the military regulations state that you cannot later change your mind and switch it to a complete CO discharge.

Third, the military regulations also state that if you in any way break conduct code or uniform standards, then you will no longer be entitled to the normal CO procedure. So it is a good time to be as respectful and law abiding as you possibly can. You don't need to run AWOL.

The military does grant a lawful honorable discharge for those who can prove a sincere change in conviction. But you must take the time to go through the proper legal channels that the regulations provide.

Applying for CO Status

The Central Committee for Conscientious Objectors has a pretty good book that helps to guide you through the whole CO process: *Advice for Conscientious Objectors in the Armed Forces*, by Robert A. Seeley.

Once you submit the application, the procedure usually is pretty standardized for most people. The steps of the process are as follows:

1. Pray.
2. Make your decision.
3. Get a copy of the regulations from your branch of the military.
4. Write out a rough draft of your convictions, stating in particular what happened to change your views since you enlisted.
5. Gather support letters from friends, family, or anyone who can testify of your convictions.
6. Get a Christian counselor to help you if you can.
7. Share your written material with your counselor.
8. Submit your complete application.
9. After you submit your application, the military is required to "make every effort" to place you on duties that conflict as little as possible with your stated beliefs. This usually means you'll be assigned to a job that doesn't involve the use of weapons.
10. Interview with a chaplain and a psychiatrist, then finally undergo a hearing with an investigative officer.
11. Wait, pray, and share your faith with others!
12. Write me a letter and tell me what the Lord has done in your life!

Alternative Service

Since the first printing of this book it has come to my attention that Christian Aid Ministries (CAM) has developed an alternative work relief program for COs in the event of a draft. The name of the program is "The Conservative Anabaptist Service Program" (CASP). Churches involved in the CASP program who have young men committed to conservative Anabaptist beliefs can register with this program and even participate in current relief work projects. For more information contact Eli Weaver at: Christian Aid Ministries, P.O. Box 360, Berlin, OH 44610. Ph: 330-893-2428.

Al·le·giance (ə-lē'jəns); from the Anglo-French word *"legaunce".* Literally translated, "loyalty of a liege-man to his lord."

1. The tie or obligation, implied or expressed, which a subject owes to his sovereign or government; the duty of fidelity to one's king, government, or state.

2. Loyalty or devotion to some person, group, cause, or the like.

3. The obligations of a servant to his lord.

Notes:

Chapter 1: Walking on Dry Ground
[1] Some of these Alamo facts are taken from Mike Cox's "Line in the sand" at http://www.texasescapes.com /MikeCoxTexasTales/ Line-in-the-Sand-Alamo-History.htm.

Chapter 3: What Changed?
[1] David Benedict, *History of the Donatists.* Providence: Nickerson, Sibley & Co., 1875, p. 39.

[2] It should be said here that at this time there also was a break off group of Donatists called the Circumcellions, which were violent in their disputes with the Catholics. Not all Donatists were Circumcellions. However, all Donatists received the persecution.

[3] The primary source is [Codex Theodosianus, 16:5, 54]. I also found it in an Encyclopedia: Simon Swain, Mark Edwards, Approaching Late Antiquity: The Transformation from Early to Late Empire. London: Oxford University Press, 2004, p. 145.

[4] G. H. Orchard, *A Concise History of the Baptists* (Chapter 2, Section 10). Nashville: Southwestern Publishing House, 1855.

[5] *Augustine of Hippo* (Epistle 93, Chapter 2). See also Allan D. Fitzgerald and John C. Cavadini, *Augustine Through the Ages: An Encyclopedia.* Grand Rapids: Wm. B. Eerdmans Publishing, p. 876.

[6] The primary source is [Augustine of Hippo, De Correct. Donatist, c. 6, § 24]. I also found this quote in: *Alonzo Trévier Jones, Civil Government and Religion: Or Christianity and the American Constitution.* Cambridge: Harvard University, 1889, p. 89.

[7] Farrar: *Lives of the Fathers.* London: Adam and Charles Black, 1907, p.536.

[8] Urban II: Speech at Council of Clermont according to Fulcher of Chartres A.D. 1095. This can be found at www.fordham.edu/halsall/source/urban2-5vers.html.

[9] Dana C. Munro, *Urban and the Crusaders, Translations and Reprints from the Original Sources of European History* (Vol. 1). Philadelphia: University of Pennsylvania, 1895.

Chapter 4: The God of the Bible

[1] Isaiah 6:1–5 NKJV
[2] R. C. Sproul, *The Holiness of God*. Wheaton, Illinois: Tyndale House Publishers Inc., 1998, p. 40.
[3] Isaiah 6:5 NKJV
[4] Exodus 33:18 NKJV
[5] Exodus 33:22 NKJV
[6] Exodus 34:5–9 KJV
[7] Exodus 34:14 KJV
[8] Hebrews 1:3 KJV
[9] Exodus 21:24; Leviticus 24:20; Deuteronomy 19:21 KJV
[10] Matthew 5:38 KJV
[11] James 1:17 NKJV
[12] Matthew 10:34–37 NKJV
[13] Hebrews 8:7–8,13 NKJV
[14] Matthew 7:28–29 NKJV
[15] Luke 9:51–56 NKJV
[16] Luke 22:35 NKJV
[17] Luke 22:35 NKJV
[18] Luke 22:35–38 NKJV
[19] Luke 22:49 KJV
[20] Matthew 26:51–53 KJV
[21] Tertullian, *On Idolatry, Ante-Nicene Fathers* (Vol. 3, p. 73). Grand Rapids: Wm. B. Eerdmans Publishing Co., 1986.

Chapter 5: The Early Church

[1] Isaiah 2:3–4 NKJV
[2] Justin Martyr, *Dialogue With Trypho, Ante-Nicene Fathers* (Vol. 1, p. 254). Grand Rapids: Wm. B. Eerdmans Publishing Co., 1986.
[3] Justin Martyr, *The First Apology of Justin, Ante-Nicene Fathers* (Vol. 1, p. 176). Grand Rapids: Wm. B. Eerdmans Publishing Co., 1986.
[4] Irenaeus, *Against Heresies, Ante-Nicene Fathers* (Vol. 1, p. 512). Grand Rapids: Wm. B. Eerdmans Publishing Co., 1986.
[5] Clement of Alexandria, *The Instructor, Book III, Ante-Nicene Fathers* (Vol. 2, p. 293). Grand Rapids: Wm. B. Eerdmans Publishing Co., 1986.

[6] Clement of Alexandria, *Exhortation to the Heathen, Ante-Nicene Fathers* (Vol. 2, p. 195). Grand Rapids: Wm. B. Eerdmans Publishing Co., 1986.

[7] Clement of Alexandria, *Maximus Sermon, Ante-Nicene Fathers* (Vol. 2, p. 581). Grand Rapids: Wm. B. Eerdmans Publishing Co., 1986.

[8] Tertullian, *An Answer To The Jews, Ante-Nicene Fathers* (Vol. 3, p. 154). Grand Rapids: Wm. B. Eerdmans Publishing Co., 1986.

[9] Tertullian, *Of Patience, Ante-Nicene Fathers* (Vol. 3, p. 711). Grand Rapids: Wm. B. Eerdmans Publishing Co., 1986.

[10] Tertullian, *Against Marcion, Ante-Nicene Fathers* (Vol. 3, p. 370). Grand Rapids: Wm. B. Eerdmans Publishing Co., 1986.

[11] Tertullian, *Apology, Ante-Nicene Fathers* (Vol. 3, p. 51). Grand Rapids: Wm. B. Eerdmans Publishing Co., 1986.

[12] Tertullian, *Of Patience, Ante-Nicene Fathers* (Vol. 3, p. 713). Grand Rapids: Wm. B. Eerdmans Publishing Co., 1986.

[13] Tertullian, *The Chaplet, Ante-Nicene Fathers* (Vol. 3, p. 100). Grand Rapids: Wm. B. Eerdmans Publishing Co., 1986.

[14] Hippolytus, *The Apostolic Tradition of Hippolytus* (Sec. 16). London: The Alban Press, 1991.

[15] Origen, *Against Celsus, Ante-Nicene Fathers* (Vol. 4, pp. 665-668, condensed). Grand Rapids: Wm. B. Eerdmans Publishing Co., 1986.

[16] Tertullian, *Apology, Ante-Nicene Fathers* (Vol. 3, p. 55). Grand Rapids: Wm. B. Eerdmans Publishing Co., 1986. Quoted from a translation taken from *Christian Research Institute Magazine, GLIMPSE* #53. (Everyone adds the phrase "of the church" to the end of this quote, so I thought I would put it in for good measure. However, please note that it is not in the original.)

[17] Origen, *Against Celsus, Ante-Nicene Fathers* (Vol. 4, p. 621). Grand Rapids: Wm. B. Eerdmans Publishing Co., 1986.

Chapter 6: The Constantine Bridge

[1] Edward Gibbon, *The History of the Decline and Fall of the Roman Empire* (Vol. 1, Ch. 37). Chicago: William Benton, 1952.

[2] Eusebius, *Ecclesiastical History, Nicene and Post-Nicene Fathers, Second Series* (Bk. 9, Ch. 9). Grand Rapids: Wm. B. Eerdmans Publishing Co., 1986.

[3] Eusebius, *Ecclesiastical History*, *Nicene and Post-Nicene Fathers, Second Series* (Bk. 1, Ch.11). Grand Rapids: Wm. B. Eerdmans Publishing Co., 1986.

[4] Eusebius, *Life of Constantine*, *Nicene and Post-Nicene Fathers, Second Series* (Bk. 3, Ch.1). Grand Rapids: Wm. B. Eerdmans Publishing Co., 1986.

[5] Eusebius, *Life of Constantine*, *Nicene and Post-Nicene Fathers, Second Series* (Bk. 3, Ch.15). Grand Rapids: Wm. B. Eerdmans Publishing Co., 1986.

[6] Justo L. Gonzalez, *The Story of Christianity, The Early Church to the Present Day,* Peabody: Prince Press, 2004, p. 123.

[7] Philip Schaff, *History of the Christian Church* (Vol. 3, p. 16). Peabody: Hendrickson Publishers, Inc., 1996.

[8] Eusebius, *Life of Constantine*, *Nicene and Post-Nicene Fathers, Second Series* (Bks. 1 and 3, Ch. 44). Grand Rapids: Wm. B. Eerdmans Publishing Co., 1986.

[9] Eusebius, *Life of Constantine*, *Nicene and Post-Nicene Fathers, Second Series* (Bk. 1, Ch. 44) Grand Rapids: Wm. B. Eerdmans Publishing Co. 1986, p. 44.

[10] Revelation 17:1–6 NKJV

[11] Tony Campolo, "Why the Church Is Important: The institutional church is for every believer." *Christianity Today* (Web-only) May, 2007 (Vol. 51).

[12] Revelation 18:4–5 NKJV

Chapter 7: Why?

[1] Gary G. Kohls "The Bombing of Nagasaki August 9, 1945: The Untold Story" at http://www.lewrockwell.com/orig5/kohls8.html.

[2] James 4:1–3 NKJV

[3] Romans 11:36 KJV

[4] Matthew 6:33 NKJV

[5] Romans 3:8 NKJV

[6] Genesis 15:1 NKJV

[7] Matthew. 6:33 NKJV

[8] Genesis 15:4 NKJV

[9] James 4:4–6 NKJV

Chapter 8: Excuses

[1] John Howard Yoder, *What Would You Do?* Scottdale: Herald Press, 1983, p. 25.

[2] John Howard Yoder, *What Would You Do?* Scottdale: Herald Press, 1983, p. 62.

[3] John Howard Yoder, *What Would You Do?* Scottdale: Herald Press, 1983, p.33.

[4] David Bercot, *The Kingdom that Turned the World Upside-Down.* Tyler: Scroll Publishing Co., 2004, p. 70.

[5] Ibid. p. 74.

Chapter 9: The Pilgrim Church

[1] Hebrews 11:13 KJV

[2] Stuart Murray, *Williams Valdes and the Early Waldensians* at http://www.anabaptistnetwork.com/ Waldensians.

[3] Peter Chelcický, *The Net of Faith.* Oberlin: Primitive Christianity, 1947.

[4] C. Vogl, *Peter Cheltschizki,em Prophet an der Wende der Zeiten.* Zuerich und Leipzig, 1926, pp. 92–94.

[5] Jonathan Dymond, *An Inquiry into the Accordancy of War.* London : Philadelphia Friends' Book Store, 1892, p. 36.

[6] Menno Simons, *Renunciation of the Church of Rome,* from *The Complete Works of Menno Simon.* Aylmer, Ontario and Lagrange, Indiana: Pathway Publishers, 1983, p.5.

[7] William Roscoe, *The Anabaptist Story: An Introduction to Sixteenth-Century Anabaptism.* Grand Rapids: Wm. B. Eerdmans Publishing Co., 1996.

[8] Menno Simons, *The Complete Works of Menno Simon* (Part II). Aylmer, Ontario and Lagrange, Indiana: Pathway Publishers, 1983, p. 170.

[9] Menno Simons, *The Complete Works of Menno Simon* (Part I). Aylmer, Ontario and Lagrange, Indiana: Pathway Publishers, 1983, p. 81.

[10] John Horsh, *The Principle of Nonresistance* at http://www.bibleviews.com/Nonresistance-Horsch.html.

[11] Mike Atnip, *How the Methodists Saved America.* Newmanstown, Pennsylvania: Primitive Christianity Publishers, p.16.

[12] Thieleman J. Van Braght, *The Martyrs Mirror.* Scottdale: Herald Press, 1990, p.741.
[13] Hebrews 12:1–2 NKJV

Chapter 10: The Two Kingdoms

[1] Matthew 22:21 KJV
[2] Acts 17:6 KJV
[3] John 18:33 NKJV
[4] John 18:34 NKJV
[5] John 18:35 NKJV
[6] John 18:36a NKJV
[7] John 18:36b NKJV
[8] John 18:37 NKJV
[9] John 18:37b NKJV
[10] John 18:37b NKJV
[11] 2 Timothy 2:3–4 NKJV
[12] Quoted from Lee c. Camp, *Mere Discipleship*, Grand Rapids, MI: Brazos Press, 2003, p. 137.

Chapter 11: Romans 13

[1] Romans 13: 1–4 NKJV
[2] John 19:3 NKJV
[3] John 19:5–6 NKJV
[4] John 19:10 NKJV
[5] John 19:10–11 NKJV
[6] Romans 13:5–7 NKJV
[7] Jeremiah 25:8–9 NKJV
[8] Jeremiah 25:12 NKJV
[9] Isaiah 44:28 NKJV
[10] Tertullian, *On Idolatry, Ante-Nicene Fathers* (Vol. 3, p. 73). Grand Rapids: Wm. B. Eerdmans Publishing Co., 1986.
[11] Romans 12:21 KJV
[12] Jeremiah 27:5–6 NKJV
[13] Daniel. 4:17 NKJV
[14] Proverbs 21:1 NJKV

Chapter 12: My Defender is God

[1] Romans 12:17–21 NKJV

[2] Tertullian, *On Prayer*, *Ante-Nicene Fathers* (Vol. 3, pp. 690–691). Grand Rapids: Wm. B. Eerdmans Publishing Co., 1986.

Chapter 13: The Theology of Martyrdom
[1] 1 Corinthians 1:18–20 NKJV
[2] Matthew 10:16 NKJV
[3] Tertullian, *Against Marcion*, *Ante-Nicene Fathers* (Vol. 3, p. 415). Grand Rapids: Wm. B. Eerdmans Publishing Co., 1986.
[4] Matthew 20:22 NKJV
[5] Matthew 20:23 NKJV
[6] Luke 9:23 NKJV
[7] Matthew 16:23-25 NJKV
[8] John 16:1–33 NKJV
[9] Philippians 1:21 KJV
[10] 2 Timothy 3:10–12 NKJV
[11] Romans 8:35–39 NKJV
[12] John 12:24 NKJV
[13] Philippians 3:10 NKJV
[14] 1 Corinthians 6:7 NKJV
[15] Romans 12:1 NKJV
[16] John D. Roth, *Choosing Against War: A Christian View*. Intercourse, PA: Good Books, 2002, p. 62–63.
[17] The Global Anabaptist Mennonite Encyclopedia at http://www.gameo.org/.
[18] Taken from Thomas Finger, *A Contemporary Anabaptist Theology* (Hans Hut, *Gospel of All Creatures*). Downers Grove, Illinois: InterVarsity Press, 2004, p.117.
[19] Maurice Roberts, "John Welsh of Ayre," *The Banner of Truth Magazine*, No. 174, March, 1978.
[20] Revelation 5:2 NKJV
[21] Revelation 5:5 NKJV
[22] Revelation 5: 6–7 NKJV
[23] Revelation 5:9–10 NKJV

Chapter 14: Him or It?
[1] Luke 12:11–12 NKJV
[2] Romans 13:4 NKJV
[3] Matthew 13:31–32 NKJV

[4] Shane Claiborne, *The Irresistible Revolution.* Grand Rapids: Zondervan, 2006, p. 336.
[5] Revelation 13:7–8 NKJV
[6] Revelation 13:10 NKJV
[7] Revelation 14:12 NKJV
[8] Matthew 26:52 NKJV
[9] Revelation 12:11 NKJV

Chapter 15: Altar Call

[1] John 18: 37 NKJV
[2] Matthew 11:12 NKJV
[3] Luke 16:16 NKJV
[4] Mark 1:14–15 KJV
[5] Romans 3:4 NKJV
[6] Mark 10:28 KJV
[7] Mark 10:20–30 KJV

Appendix

[1] 1 Peter 4:17 NKJV
[2] MO 1306.16E paragraph C

About the Author

Dean Taylor lives in Ephrata, Pennsylvania, with his wife Tania and their six children: Stephen, Stephana, Christian, Christina, Joanna, and John Wesley. He is the associate pastor of Living Hope Christian Fellowship. He is also editor of "The Heartbeat of the Remnant."

For information about evangelism, church, or group discount prices, please contact our distributer at:

Scroll Publishing Company
P.O. Box 122
Amberson, PA 17210.

(717) 349-7033
www.Scrollpublishing.com

For new books and other information from Radical Reformation Books, you may visit our website at:

www.RadicalReformation.com

Filling out the Selective Service card:

Declaration of Conscientious Objection to War

I have included a postcard taken directly from the form that the Selective Service sends you at the time of a draft (SSS Form 22). Simply fill out this card and mail it to yourself.

Please understand that there is nothing "official" that happens by sending in this card. However, by mailing this card to yourself, you will have proof that you held a conviction against war before a draft begins.

Getting it notarized would be icing on the cake, but at the very least, a stamp and dated post card would be a choice thing to have when you face your draft board meeting.

The second statement, which states that you will be asking for an "exemption from all training and service as a member of the armed Forces (Class I-O)," simply means that you object to all wars and desire not to participate in the military in any way—combatant or non-combatant.

The final statement points to the fact that your convictions are based on a relationship with Jesus Christ.